# Derivative Instruments

# Derivative Instruments

### Editor

### *Edward J. Swan*

## Graham & Trotman / Martinus Nijhoff
Members of the Kluwer Academic Publishers Group
LONDON/DORDRECHT/BOSTON

Graham & Trotman Limited
Sterling House
66 Wilton Road
London SW1V 1DE
UK

Kluwer Academic Publishers Group
101 Philip Drive
Assinippi Park
Norwell, MA 02061
USA

© Institute of Advanced Legal Studies 1994
First published 1994

**British Library Cataloguing in Publication Data is available**

ISBN : 1-85966-057-6

**Library of Congress Cataloguing-in-Publication Data**
Derivative instruments / edited by Edward J. Swan.
    p.  cm.
    On t.p.: Institute of Advanced Legal Studies.
    "Papers presented ... at the prestigious International Conference
on Derivative Instruments at London University's Institute of
Advanced Legal Studies in October 1993"–CIP galley introd.
    Includes index.
    ISBN 1-85966-057-6
    1. Derivative securities–Congresses.  I. Swan, Edward J.
II. University of London. Institute of Advanced Legal Studies.
III. International Conference on Derivative Instruments (1993:
London, England)
    K1331.A55   1993
    346 092–dc20                        94-8105
    [346.692]                             CIP

Computer typeset in Times by BookEns Ltd, Baldock, Herts.
Printed and bound in Great Britain by Hartnolls Ltd, Bodmin, Cornwall.

# Contents

### Acknowledgements

On pp. 140 and 151 figures are reproduced from *Chaos and Order in the Capital Markets* by Edgar E. Peters: © Copyright John Wiley & Sons Inc., 1991.

On p. 150 a figure is adapted with permission of the *Financial Analysts Journal,* November/December 1992. Copyright 1992, Association for Investment Management and Research, Charlottesville, Va. All rights reserved.

# INTRODUCTION

Derivative instruments are the contracts used in perhaps the world's biggest market, the market for future commodities. The total value of those contracts probably exceeds two trillion US dollars per day. However, this business is, at present, almost totally unknown to the public at large. Only a few well-informed financial specialists are aware of its nature, its size, and its implications for the future direction of the world economy. Very little of substance has been published about this critically important business. Consequently, this book is a seminal work on derivative instruments, containing the current views of the world's leading regulators, most successful traders, and top legal, economic and scientific experts.

This book is a collection of the papers presented by the world's leading regulators and experts in derivative instruments at the prestigious International Conference on Derivative Instruments at London University's Institute of Advanced Legal Studies in October 1993. Presenting papers to an audience of sophisticated financial and legal experts were regulators including the head of the United States' Commodity Futures Trading Commission (CFTC) and the UK's Securities and Futures Authority (SFA); the economic adviser of the principal monitor of derivative instrument trading Switzerland's Bank for International Settlements; the managing director of the most successful derivatives trader, Bankers Trust Company of New York; a top scientific expert on mathematical modelling; and leading regulatory and litigation lawyers in the field from the United States and the United Kingdom.

At the time of writing this information is the latest thinking from those intimately involved with making the enormous derivative instrument business run smoothly, profitably, and beneficially to the nations that host it.

The first chapter is by Pauline Ashall, a partner with the distinguished London solicitors firm, Linklaters & Paines. She writes about the increasingly important topic of EC regulation of derivative instruments. This topic is of growing importance, not only because the regulations of the UK and other EC countries will be increasingly similar, but also because the nature of the derivative instrument markets is that they are international, and consequently extremely difficult to regulate with purely national regulatory systems. Some kind of international regulation is essential to keep track of this huge market with implications for the world's economy. Consequently, co-operative regulation by nations is becoming more important, and regulation of this business by the EC nations will continue to be important to understand because a large percentage of the world's derivatives business is done in Europe.

The second chapter is by the world's most powerful regulator of futures and derivatives trading, Sheila Bair, acting Chairman of the US Commodity Futures Trading Commission (CFTC). More futures and derivatives trading is done in the United States than in any other jurisdiction, but in recent years its share of this business has been declining, and much of that business has been migrating overseas to London and other European trading centres to take advantage of less complex regulation and lower transactions costs. Acutely aware of this flight of business, the US government has been taking steps to liberalise its regulations to make it easier to do futures and derivatives transactions in the United States, particularly transactions in markets dominated by large volume commercial traders such as the swaps and energy markets. Commissioner Bair outlines the CFTC approach to regulation, its attempts to streamline US regulation to make it more responsive to the needs of modern financial markets, and its plans for the future.

Chapter 3 is by Dr. Horst Bockelmann, economic adviser to Switzerland's Bank for International Settlements (BIS), which has for many years been the principal monitor of the size and nature of the derivative instruments business, in which large international banks are probably the most important participants. Dr. Bockelmann is one of the key observers and commentators on this business. The fruit of his long and detailed study of this subject is contained in his chapter which is an up-to-date analysis of the size of the market, and the problems it could pose for the financial health of the nations that host this trade.

The fourth chapter is by Richard Farrant, the new Chief Executive of the UK's Securities and Futures Authority, and previously Deputy Head of Banking Supervision for the Bank of England. Recognising the importance of international regulation, he outlines the measures that need to be adopted in order to make it work effectively without jeopardising the prosperity of the business. Mr. Farrant points out that the integrity of these markets require the support of policies to increase the technical knowledge of the traders, to permit netting of traders' positions in order to reduce risk, and better reporting of the levels of trade and exposure in the derivative markets. As one of the most important regulators in derivatives, his views command serious attention.

The fifth chapter is by Dr. Kenneth Garbade, managing director of Bankers Trust Company of New York. The profitability of Bankers Trust in recent years is the principal success story of derivatives instruments trading. Under the supervision of forward-thinking executives like Dr. Garbade, Bankers Trust refocused its business in the late 1980s to become one of the pioneers in expanding the derivative instruments market. Their enormous success has made them one of the leaders of, and most respected traders in these markets. In his chapter, Dr. Garbade gives some insight into one of the basic methods used by Bankers Trust to value the assets of client companies for purposes of writing derivative instrument financing.

Chapter 6 is by Alan Newton, a partner in Freshfields, one of the leading firms of banking and financial services solicitors in the UK. This chapter provides an excellent overview of legal and regulatory developments affecting the derivatives business in the UK, covering such issues as contract formation, security and documentation.

The seventh chapter deals with the issue of competition

between market centres for the lucrative derivative instrument business, drawing on the author's many years as a US lawyer involved in research and litigation on derivative instrument issues. The size and importance of this business makes it increasingly desirable to attract to competing market centres. This chapter explores the nature of the business, and how regulatory thinking should be framed in order to persuade the trading community to do their business in a particular national jurisdiction. An examination of the competitive edge gained in recent years by the UK over the markets of the United States is explored. This chapter concludes with suggestions as to how developing and newly emerging nations might be able to compete for parts of the derivative instrument business in the future.

Chapter 8 is a remarkable explanation of the technical complexities of the type of mathematical modelling used to help calculate the risks involved in writing derivative instruments. Professor Vvedensky is a solid state physicist at Imperial College, London, and is in a unique position to offer an outside mathematical expert's opinion of the methods used by financial institutions to calculate the range of their investment risks in these markets. In the past, when explanations of this aspect of the derivative instrument market have been given, they have usually been so impenetrably technical that non-mathematicians have been able to understand them only with the greatest difficulty. In this chapter, Professor Vvedensky takes an entirely different approach, explaining complex concepts in ordinary language understandable by laymen. The result is that anyone involved in the derivative instrument business now has clearer access to the technical side of the business.

The final chapter is by one of the UK's leading experts on derivative instruments, Philip Wood, a partner in the large London solicitors form of Allen & Overy. Mr. Wood's topic is the uses of 'netting' in financial markets. Netting is the ability to set off reciprocal claims in the event of the insolvency of a party to a transaction. The circumstances under which this can be done in various legal jurisdictions has become a controversial issue in the field of derivative instrument regulation because the practice, although it greatly reduces the risks of derivative instrument trading, often conflicts with bankruptcy laws. Mr. Wood provides a clear explanation of the different methods of netting, how it is applied in England, how it is treated in a number of other countries, and why the derivative instrument business would be more secure if netting were accepted more widely.

In summary this book covers a variety of important issues that bear on the enormous market of derivative instrument trading. The size and continued growth of this sector of the financial services business means that an increasing number of lawyers, government and market regulators, and financial services industry employees will have to have a solid understanding of how derivative instrument trading works and what issues it raises. This volume contains the explanations of the most knowledgeable experts and is the best primary source for newcomers to begin to learn about derivative instruments or for an experienced practitioners to expand their understanding.

Edward J. Swan
Editor
Institute of Advanced Legal Studies
University of London
17 April 1994

*Chapter 1*

# EC REGULATION AND DERIVATIVES

Pauline Ashall,
Linklaters & Paines

## 1. INTRODUCTION

A key part of a single European market is the liberalisation of the capital markets in the EC. The EC financial services industry is a significant industry in its own right, representing about 7 per cent of economic activity within the Community. More importantly, European trade generally requires free access to financial services, including sources of finance. However, as seen in the UK, deregulation, in the sense of removal of restrictions on competition, also tends to bring with it additional regulation of the players in the liberalised market. At EC level, the Single Market Programme includes numerous Directives designed to achieve harmonisation of standards for the authorisation and ongoing supervision of the financial services industry. This has been accompanied by other Directives designed to prevent market abuses such as insider dealing and money laundering. Only on the basis of this additional regulation are banks, investment firms and insurance companies to be given additional freedoms to provide their services throughout the EC. These freedoms are usually referred to as the 'passports'. While there are no Directives devoted exclusively to derivatives and the derivatives industry, derivatives are an important part of the capital markets and, as such, are within the scope of the various Directives.

The impact of EC regulation on derivatives can be broken down into the following main areas:

1

(i)   the regulation of entities dealing in derivatives. This includes requirements for authorisation, capital and conduct of business;

(ii)  increased opportunities for dealing in derivatives across national borders. This includes access to derivatives exchanges in other member states; and

(iii) briefly, some other ways in which EC regulation may impact on derivatives, such as use of derivatives by investment funds.

## 2. REGULATION OF DERIVATIVES BUSINESS

In the United Kingdom, derivatives business can be conducted either by a bank or by another type of investment firm. In either case, authorisation under the Financial Services Act is required. In some continental European countries, financial services tend to be concentrated in banking entities the so-called universal banks.

### 2.1 Banks: authorisation

Regulation of banks at EC level is now very well developed, with harmonised minimum standards for authorisation required by the First Banking Co-Ordination Directive, and somewhat expanded in the Second Banking Co-Ordination Directive. These Directives also require the banking authorities in the bank's home state to monitor the bank's activities on an ongoing basis. From 1996, banks which conduct financial services activities, including financial derivatives business, will also be subject to the conduct of business requirements in the Investment Services Directive.

### 2.2 Investment firms: authorisation

In contrast to banks, there are currently no EC-wide standards for authorisation and monitoring of the activities of non-bank investment firms, including those conducting derivatives business. This will change from 1 January 1996, when EC member states are required to implement the Investment Services Directive (ISD) and the Capital Adequacy Directive (CAD). Investment firms dealing in financial derivatives will need to obtain authorisation under the ISD in their home state. This applies across a wide range of instruments, from currency options to interest rate swaps to OTC equity derivatives. Commodities derivatives, however, are not within the scope of the ISD, or the Second Banking Directive.

The ISD lays down requirements for authorisation of an investment firm, together with certain ongoing regulatory requirements. These requirements will also apply to banks conducting investment services. The Capital Adequacy Directive will lay down minimum initial capital requirements for investment firms. It will also impose risk-based capital requirements for the trading book of both banks and investment firms.

I now want to look briefly at the likely impact of these Directives, firstly in the area of capital, and secondly conduct of business.

## 2.3 Banks: capital

The minimum initial capital for a bank, as set out in the Second Banking Directive, is ECU 5 million. What is more important, there is a series of Directives on the capital that a bank must maintain to meet the risks inherent in its business. Broadly, the Solvency Ratio Directive requires banks to maintain own funds of at least 8 per cent of risk-weighted assets. This is intended to ensure that banks have sufficient capital to withstand the credit risks inherent in their business.

How the risk-weighting for derivatives are calculated is complex, with a distinction being made between interest and foreign exchange related instruments, and other off-balance sheet derivatives. Most banks which actively deal in interest rate and foreign exchange contracts will mark them to market and apply the relevant risk-weightings to the current replacement value. In calculating the capital requirements, netting of exposures to a counterparty is only recognised in very limited circumstances, namely bilateral netting by novation.

## 2.4 Investment firms: capital

Turning to investment firms, from January 1996 the Capital Adequacy Directive will require investment firms to have minimum initial capital. It will also impose capital requirements on both banks and investment firms in respect of the market risks in their 'trading book'.

## 2.5 The trading book

The 'trading book' is broadly defined to cover proprietary positions taken for trading purposes in financial instruments. Financial instruments has the meaning set out in the Investment Services Directive. The definition will include all kinds of derivatives based on an underlying investment, on interest rates and currencies. The trading book also includes stocklending transactions, repos and reverse repos.

In respect of their trading books, both banks and investment firms must meet capital requirements intended to cover against position risks, settlement and counterparty risks, and large exposures. The capital requirements for position risks are based on the so-called building block methodology, with a general risk weighing for the type of instrument and a specific risk weighing for the particular issuer. In calculating the position risk requirements, netting is permitted in respect of long and short positions in the same instrument. Also, positions in the underlying instruments can be offset against derivative positions in relation to those instruments. This is more flexible than the approach currently taken for banks in the Solvency Ratio Directive. The CAD does not allow, in calculating the capital requirements, for netting of exposures with the same counterparty relating to different instruments. However, it is likely that the CAD will be amended in due course to reflect the latest Basle Proposals on bilateral netting, which were published in April 1993.

In respect of the capital requirements for the trading book only, the types of capital which can be counted towards the requirements are more extensive than is otherwise the case. For example, within certain limits, short-term subordinated debt will count as capital for this purpose.

In general, the CAD is likely to result in increased capital requirements. Under the CAD, similar rules will apply to banks and investment firms conducting the same business, achieving a more level playing field. Since the Basle Proposals on market risk and interest rate risk are similar to the CAD, similar standards are also likely to be introduced for non-EC banks and investment firms.

## 2.6 Banks and investment firms: conduct of business

Turning to ongoing requirements of conduct, the ISD will require the authorities in each state to impose prudential rules on banks and investment firms authorised by that state. These will cover matters such as record-keeping, safe custody and accounting procedures. The Directive also requires states to draw up conduct of business rules covering matters such as conflicts of interest, best execution and advertising. Pending further harmonisation, the rules to be applied are those of the state in which the services are performed.

All these requirements will apply to banks and investment firms set up in an EC member state to conduct derivatives business, even if their business is only conducted in that state and not cross-border. For entities set up in the UK, this is likely to result in fairly minor changes to the existing requirements under the Financial Services Act. In some other states it will be necessary to set up a whole new regulatory framework to comply with the Directives.

## 2.7 Other Directives

Other Directives may have a significant impact on the way in which derivatives firms conduct their business. The Insider Dealing Directive extends to dealings, either on regulated markets or through a professional intermediary, in a wide range of instruments, including options, warrants and futures contracts relating to transferable securities. Derivatives relating to an index based on transferable securities, such as the FTSE 100 index, are also within the scope of the Directive. The Directive is shortly to be implemented in the UK by the Criminal Justice Act. This considerably expands the scope of the previous insider dealing legislation in respect of derivatives.

Another important Directive is the prevention of the use of the financial system for the purposes of money laundering. Banks and investment firms will need to have in place procedures for identification of their customers and for monitoring of transactions which could involve money laundering. This will apply to derivatives transactions in the same way as their other business.

## 3. THE PASSPORT

We have just looked briefly at the regulatory standards which will apply throughout the EC for establishing and operating a bank or investment firm which conducts derivatives business. That's the bad news: the good news is that a bank or investment firm which is authorised in its home state will have a 'passport' to provide its activities throughout the EC, on the basis of its home state authorisation.

### 3.1 Scope of the passport-banks

Since 1 January 1993 banks have had a 'passport' under the Second Banking Co-Ordination Directive. In limited circumstances, the passport is also available to their subsidiaries. The passport covers all the activities listed in the Annex to the Second Banking Directive, so long as the bank's authorisation in its home state covers all those activities. For convenience, UK banks are deemed to be authorised as banks to conduct all these activities, even though they also need to become authorised under the Financial Services Act for many of the activities.

With regard to the activities for which the 'passport' is

available, the Directive does not further define what is meant by 'financial futures and options', 'transferable securities' and 'exchange and interest rate instruments'. There is clearly some overlap between these categories. The UK Treasury has issued some guidance comparing the activities covered by the Directive and the activities covered by the Financial Services Act. The main point is that while commodities derivatives may be caught by the FSA, they are not covered by the Directive and so the 'passport' is not available for them.

## 3.2 Scope of the passport-investment firms

From 1996 investment firms will need to be authorised for the purposes of the Investment Services Directive if they conduct the activities in Section A of the Annex to the ISD. Confusingly, the terms used are not identical to those in the Second Banking Directive. Also, the ISD (unlike the Second Banking Directive), seeks to define terms such as 'transferable securities'. However, in the context of derivatives, it is unlikely that there will be any difference in practice between the scope of the 'passport' under the two Directives.

In each case, commodities derivatives are not covered. On the one hand, this may be convenient for firms which just deal in commodities, such as some London Metal Exchange members. They will not be within the scope of the ISD and so will not be subject to the attendant authorisation and capital requirements. On the other hand, the result of excluding commodities derivatives may be unsatisfactory. For example, a French bank can trade in equity derivatives in London on the basis of the 'passport'. However if it wants to write gold options, or trade in oil products on the International Petroleum Exchange it will have to seek separate authorisation for this under the Financial Services Act, as it is outside the scope of the 'passport'.

## 3.3 Implications of the passport

Where the 'passport' is available, what is this likely to mean in practice? The firm will be free to set up a branch in another

EC state or provide services there on a cross-border basis. It will not be necessary to obtain local authorisation or to set up a locally incorporated subsidiary. Instead, before setting up the branch or providing the services, it will have to comply with the notification procedures laid down under the relevant Directive. This broadly means notifying its home state authorities, which will, if satisfied that the firm should be able to conduct those activities, notify the host state regulators. While the host state regulators must allow the firm to conduct the activities in that state, they can impose conduct of business requirements on the firm's activities in that state, so long as these requirements can be justified in the 'general good'.

There are a number of difficult issues here. There is concern that a firm providing services throughout the EC will be subjected to separate conduct of business requirements in each state. This could considerably hamper the development of the Single European Market. Under the Directives, host state rules can only be imposed where a branch has been set up, or where services are being provided in that state on a cross-border basis. If a bank in London agrees by telephone to enter into an interest rate swap with a company in France, is the UK bank providing a service in France, or in the UK? The issue of cross-border activities is under discussion at the Commission, but no clear answer has emerged.

The other issue is that the host state regulations must be in the 'general good'. This means that the regulations must not duplicate home state requirements, must not be discriminatory and must not impose burdens out of proportion to the benefits they are designed to achieve. However, in practice, host states are tending to impose some detailed requirements. For example, a French bank which conducts a derivatives business from London and Paris will be subject to all the relevant conduct of business rules of the Securities and Futures Authority in respect of the activities of the London branch and will be subject to different regulatory requirements in respect of activities in Paris.

## 3.4 Derivatives exchanges

While banks already have the 'passport' in respect of derivatives business, one major limitation is that the 'passport' does not entitle banks to membership of derivatives exchanges within the EC. This may be a major restriction, since many exchanges, for example Marché à Terme International de France (MATIF) in France, will only grant membership to entities incorporated and capitalised locally. A further problem is that, even if an exchange is willing to allow banks or investment firms based in another country to participate in trading on the exchange, for example by having a dealing screen, this may conflict with regulatory requirements in that country. For example, there has recently been discussion with the UK authorities as to whether, if firms in London have access to DTB (Deutsche Termin-boerse) trading screens, this would require the DTB to become a recognised investment exchange in the UK.

This will all change when the Investment Services Directive is implemented. From that point, derivatives exchanges must be prepared to grant membership to banks and investment firms from other member states. Also, if an exchange in one country wishes to offer dealing facilities to firms based in another member state, the latter cannot prevent this.

# 4. OTHER ASPECTS OF EC REGULATION

So far, I have concentrated on the regulation of the firms which deal in derivatives, and the opportunities for them to provide their services cross-border. Of course, depending on the types of product concerned, and the types of investor at which they are targeted, other aspects of EC regulation may be relevant.

## 4.1 Listing and prospectuses

First, some products which are regarded as derivatives also fall within the definition of 'securities', for example index-linked bonds. If a listing is to be obtained for the product in question, then the relevant listing requirements will need to be complied with, including publication of listing particulars. The laws of each state must reflect the harmonised minimum requirements of the various Directives on listing.

A product such as an index-linked bond which is not listed, but is to be marketed to the public, will need to be marketed in accordance with a prospectus complying with the Public Offers Directive. This has not yet been fully implemented in the UK, although the UK will grant mutual recognition to prospectuses issued in other member states which meet the requirements of this Directive.

## 4.2 Undertaking for collective investment in Transferable Securities (UCITS)

The entity to which a derivative product is being marketed may itself be subject to EC-based regulation. One example is a fund which has been established to comply with the UCITS Directive, so that the fund is eligible to be marketed throughout the EC.

At present, such a fund can only be set up to invest in transferable securities. The UCITS Directive provides that funds may be allowed to employ techniques intended to provide protection against exchange risk, and also to adopt other techniques such as hedging, so long as this is for the purpose of efficient portfolio management. The leeway this gives a fund to use derivatives is extremely unclear. Not surprisingly, different states applied the Directive in different ways. There is now a proposal for a further Directive which, among other things, would amend the UCITS Directive to permit the use of financial derivatives so long as the exposures covered by assets in the fund-gearing is not permitted. This may be a significant improvement on the present position.

## 5. CONCLUSION

In summary, it can be seen that most of the regulatory requirements for running a derivatives business stem from EC-based initiatives. Further reforms in the future are also likely to emerge from Brussels rather than from national authorities. Therefore, the importance of monitoring EC developments cannot be overstressed.

It will not be clear before 1996 at the earliest how far the Single Market reforms will in fact change the derivatives markets in Europe. However, businesses need to give very careful consideration to the new opportunities.

*Chapter 2*

# UNITED STATES REGULATION OF DERIVATIVE INSTRUMENTS: REFLECTIONS FROM A CRUCIAL CROSSROADS

## Sheila Bair, Acting Chairman,[1] Commodity Futures Trading Commission

Regulation of derivative instruments in the United States stands at a crucial crossroads. Ideas and proposals are being discussed which could significantly alter the regulatory structure for both exchange traded and over-the-counter derivatives. At the same time, the Commodity Futures Trading Commission (CFTC), the futures market regulator, awaits the arrival of three new Commissioners, a new working majority appointed by the Clinton Administration. The CFTC is also soon to undergo its fifth Congressional reauthorisation. Hearings should begin early in 1994, with debate over the regulatory treatment of derivatives sure to play a prominent role in the deliberations. This paper will explore the rather convoluted paths that have brought US derivatives regulation to this critical juncture and take a look down some of the roads that lie open before it.

## 1. ORIGINS OF THE US FUTURES REGULATORY SYSTEM

Federal regulation of futures markets in the United States

1. The views expressed in this paper are those of the author and do not necessarily reflect those of the Commodity Futures Trading Commission. The author is appreciative to Don Heitman of the Commodity Futures Trading Commission for his assistance in preparing this paper.

actually predates federal securities regulation, tracing its
origins back to the Grain Futures Act of 1922.[2] The historical
antecedents of today's regulatory system arose in the context
of purely agricultural futures markets, suffering from the
depredations of 'bucket shops' – brokerage enterprises which
would take the opposite side of customer orders without
executing them on an exchange. If the customers guessed
wrong, the bucket shop operators pocketed the profits. If too
many guessed right, they disappeared into the night leaving
the customers holding worthless contracts.

The legislative response to this problem was an 'exchange
trading requirement', which has remained enshrined in US
law ever since. It provides that futures contracts may legally
be traded only on a contract market designated as such under
the Commodity Exchange Act.[3] Thus, while US law has
always recognised and regulated off-exchange trading of
securities, off-exchange futures trading was (and is) illegal.
Designated exchanges have enjoyed a statutory monopoly on
futures trading.

This regulatory approach worked well for a long time, but
over the last 20 years or so it has been quite thoroughly
overtaken by events. Beginning in the early 1970s, regulated
futures markets enjoyed an explosion of growth with the
development of financial futures and options. At the same
time, the over-the-counter (OTC) markets were also blossom-
ing with a variety of new risk-shifting products – hybrid
instruments which combined the features of traditional debt
or equity instruments with futures or options-like components, as well as swaps and other products. Many of these
new OTC products resemble futures both in design and in the
economic functions they perform. However, unlike the bucket
shops at which the exchange trading requirement was aimed,
these products fulfil a legitimate economic need for legitimate
market users.

2. Stat. 998 (1922), 7 USC sections *et seq.*
3. Commodity Exchange Act section 4(a), 7 USC section 6 (1982).

# 2. CFTC REGULATION OF OTC DERIVATIVES

The CFTC, which came into existence in 1974, has struggled mightily in seeking to apply an inflexible statute to innovative financial products which the law's drafters clearly never envisioned. Initially, the agency took a hands-off approach to these new products. However, as the OTC derivatives market grew, it eventually became too big to ignore. In 1987 the CFTC brought an injunctive action against Wells Fargo Bank NA charging that the 'Gold Market Certificate' Wells Fargo had recently begun marketing was, in essence, a cash settled option in violation of agency regulations against off-exchange options. The resulting Consent Order rescinded all the gold market certificates that had been sold and directed the bank to refund customers' money with interest. That same year, the agency began an investigation into the swaps market activities of the Chase Manhattan Bank. The Commission's investigation caused the suspension of most domestic swap activity and, in effect, forced the swaps business overseas.

The agency, however, was neither blind to the economic issues raised by off-exchange products nor deaf to the criticism its enforcement actions were generating. In June 1987 the Commission appointed an Off-Exchange Task Force of Commission staff members to study, among other things, the public policy issues these transactions raised and the jurisdiction of the CFTC and other regulatory agencies over them. The Task Force made a preliminary report to the Commission later that year and in 1988 began issuing no-action letters, on a case-by-case basis, regarding specific off-exchange instruments.

After gathering comments through an Advance Notice of Proposed Rulemaking,[4] the Commission proceeded to more broad-based actions. In January 1989 the Commission published a statutory interpretation recognising an outright exclusion from regulation for certain categories of hybrid instruments.[5] At the same time, it published a request for

---

4. 52 Fed. Reg. 47022 (11 Dec. 1987).
5. 54 Fed. Reg. 1139 (11 Jan. 1989).

comment on proposed rules to exempt an additional category of hybrids, with limited option components, that may otherwise be considered subject to CFTC regulatory authority.[6] In July 1989 the Commission published final rules establishing the hybrids exemption.[7] On the same day, the Commission issued a policy statement creating a 'safe harbour' from regulation for most swaps trading.[8]

For a time, these CFTC actions brought some comfort to market participants concerned about possible legal challenges to the enforceability of swaps and other OTC derivative products. However, the spectre of the exchange trading requirement remained. There was always the possibility that a counterparty on the losing end of a transaction, faced with large market losses, would argue that the transaction was an off-exchange futures transaction and, as such, was illegal and unenforceable.

In 1990, that very situation arose in another OTC venue, the market for Brent crude oil forwards, commonly known as 15-day Brent contracts. A party to one of these contracts was successful in convincing a federal district court that the contracts were, indeed, off-exchange futures and therefore unenforceable.[9] The Brent market was thrown into confusion and it became difficult for US firms to find willing foreign counterparties in Brent forward transactions. The CFTC attempted to clarify matters by promptly issuing a Statutory Interpretation[10] stating that the 15-day Brent contracts were excluded from regulation under the 'forwards exclusion' of the Commodity Exchange Act (CEA or 'the Act') as a 'sale of [a] cash commodity for deferred shipment or delivery'.[11] A cloud of legal uncertainty lingered, however, and it remained difficult for US firms to participate in the 15-day Brent market.

6. 54 Fed. Reg. 1128 (11 Jan. 1989).
7. 54 Fed. Reg. 30684 (21 July 1989).
8. 54 Fed. Reg. 30694 (21 July 1989).
9. *Transnor (Bermuda) Limited v BP North America Petroleum*, 783 F. Supp. 1472 (SDNY 1990).
10. 55 Fed. Reg. 39188 (25 Sep. 1990).

# 3. STATUTORY CHANGES

The Commission was being forced into ever more tortured interpretations of the Commodity Exchange Act in order to avoid economically disrupting the new OTC derivatives markets. How was it to resolve this conflict between the ongoing development of legitimate OTC risk management products and the statutory monopoly of the exchange trading requirement? The logical solution was to amend the statute to clarify the legal status of swaps and other OTC derivative instruments. The opportunity for such a legislative fix presented itself in the agency's fourth Congressional reauthorisation, a contentious process that began with hearings in early 1989 and finally concluded with enactment of the Futures Trading Practices Act of 1992 (FTPA) in October 1992.[12]

The initial response to the CFTC's legislative efforts was a package of jurisdictional amendments contained in Title III of the Senate reauthorisation bill. These included both a specific regulatory exemption for swaps and a broad grant of general exemptive authority. The general exemptive authority went well beyond the exchange trading issue. It would allow the Commission to exempt *any* transaction or class of transactions from *any* provision of the Commodity Exchange Act, either unconditionally or on stated terms, subject to a 'public interest' test and other specified standards.[13]

Title III ran into strong opposition in the House of Representatives. The regulated futures exchanges complained that the swaps exemption gave OTC products an unfair competitive advantage over exchange-traded contracts. Eventually, the mandatory swaps exemption was dropped

11. Commodity Exchange Act, section 1a(11), 7 USC section 1a (1992).
12. Pub. L. 102–546, 106 Stat. 3590 (1992).
13. The exemptive authority had one other limitation. It did not extend to Section 2(a)(1)(B) of the Act, the so-called Johnson–Shad Accord, named for the chairmen of the CFTC and the SEC, respectively, who negotiated it. The Accord delineates the jurisdictional boundaries between the two agencies in the areas of futures and options on stocks and stock indices.

from the bill. The broad grant of discretionary exemptive authority, however, was retained.

The exemptive authority's public interest test, in addition to considering 'the national public interests noted in the Act', was intended to include, 'the prevention of fraud and the preservation of the financial integrity of markets . . .'[14] Any exemption must also be subject to the conditions that the exempted transactions will not have a 'material adverse effect' on the ability of the Commission or any exchange to 'discharge its regulatory or self-regulatory duties' and 'will be entered into solely between appropriate persons'.[15] 'Appropriate persons' are defined in the statute generally to include institutional or professional traders, but also 'such other persons that the Commission determines to be appropriate in light of their financial or other qualifications, or the applicability of appropriate regulatory protections'.[16]

However, the legislative guidance on just how Congress expected the CFTC to use this new authority was something less than a model of clarity. At one point, the conference report on the FTPA states that,

> The goal of providing the Commission with broad exemptive powers is not to prompt a wide-scale deregulation of markets falling within the ambit of the Act. Rather, it is to give the Commission a means of providing certainty and stability to existing and emerging markets so that financial innovation and market development can proceed in an effective and competitive manner.[17]

On the other hand, the conferees also stated that the grant of general exemptive authority,

> . . . is intended to promote responsible economic and financial innovation and fair competition. . . . [T]he Commission, in considering fair competition, will implement this provision in

14. H.R. Rep. No. 978, 102d Cong., 2d Sess. 78 (1992).
15. Commodity Exchange Act, section 4(c)(2)(B), 7 USC section 6(c)(2)(B) (1992).
16. ID at section 4(c)(3)(K).
17. H.R. Rep. No. 978, at 81.

a fair and even-handed manner to products and systems sponsored by exchanges and non-exchanges alike.[18]

In other words, the Commission is to provide existing OTC markets with legal certainty, so that they can develop and innovation can proceed, while neither giving OTC markets an undue competitive advantage, nor commencing a wide-scale deregulation of the regulated exchange markets – not exactly a simple task. The conference report specifically stated that the Commission was 'expect[ed] and strongly encourage[d]' to 'use its new exemptive powers promptly' in several areas 'where significant concerns of legal uncertainty have arisen'.[19] The areas specifically mentioned in the conference report included hybrids, swaps and 'forwards', with a specific citation to the *Transnor* case. The Commission wasted no time in exercising this new authority.

## 4. THE SWAPS EXEMPTION

Two weeks after the reauthorisation bill was signed into law, the Commission proposed an exemption for swaps transactions.[20] In January 1993 it approved final rules to implement a swaps exemption.[21] The exemption employs the US Bankruptcy Code's fairly broad definition of 'swap agreement', (which had been incorporated by reference into the reauthorisation legislation).[22] Eligible swap participants are generally restricted to the list of 'appropriate persons' in

18. Id at 78.
19. Id. at 81.
20. 57 Fed. Reg. 53627 (12 Nov. 1992).
21. 58 Fed. Reg. 5587 (22 Jan. 1993).
22. USC section 101(55). Swap transaction means (a) an agreement (including terms and conditions incorporated by reference therein) which is a rate swap agreement, basis swap, forward rate agreement, commodity swap, interest rate option, forward foreign exchange agreement, rate cap agreement, rate floor agreement, rate collar agreement, currency swap agreement, cross-currency rate swap agreement, currency option, any other similar agreement (including any option to enter into any of the foregoing); (b) any combination of the foregoing; or (c) a master agreement for the foregoing together with all supplements.

Section 4(c)(3) of the Act, but the Commission used its discretionary authority to tighten some of the criteria for appropriate persons listed in the statute (*eg*, the asset test for employee benefit plans was increased to US$5 million) and to designate additional 'appropriate persons' (eg, natural persons with US$10 million in assets).

The final rules include three further conditions generally seen as providing a basis for distinguishing between exempted swaps and traditional futures transactions. First, swap agreements 'may not be part of a fungible class of agreements that are standardised as to their material economic terms'.[23] The intent is to make clear that the exemption does not extend to the creation of a market in fixed term swap agreements which functions essentially the same way as an exchange except for the bilateral execution of transactions. Second, the creditworthiness of any party with an actual or potential obligation under an exempt swap must be a 'material consideration in entering into or determining the terms of the swap agreement'.[24] Third, the swaps may not be traded on a 'multilateral transaction execution facility', described more fully as '. . . a physical or electronic facility in which all market makers and other participants . . . simultaneously have the ability to execute transactions and bind both parties by accepting offers which are made by one member and open to all members of the facility'.[25]

The exchanges had objected to the original swaps proposal on several grounds. One particularly forceful (and in my view, correct) argument held that the proposal arbitrarily disadvantaged futures style clearing systems by excluding clearing systems which mutualise risk, while apparently allowing other types of centralised clearing that might rely on letters of credit or third party insurance to guarantee payment. The Federal Reserve Board had also commented in favour of a more receptive position regarding 'appropriately

23. 58 Fed. Reg. 5587 at 5590.
24. Id.
25. Id. at 5591.

structured multilateral payment netting and settlement facilities'.[26]

The final rules were revised to distinguish between bilateral and multilateral netting arrangements. In respect of the former, the rules permit 'bilateral arrangements for the netting of obligations to make payments or transfers of property, including margin or collateral'.[27] Multiparty netting is also allowed, but only to the extent that 'the underlying gross obligations among the parties are not extinguished until all netting obligations are fully performed'.[28] In other words, a multilateral facility could perform processing and book-keeping functions, but could not assume the role of a centralised counterparty and assume the net obligations of market participants.

The final rules also make clear, however, that the CFTC would welcome exemption applications for both clearing and transaction execution facilities for swaps. In fact, one footnote states that,

> The Commission believes that a clearing house system for swap agreements could be beneficial to participants and the public generally ... [and] will consider the terms and conditions of such an exemption for swap clearing houses in the context of specific proposals from exchanges, other regulators or others.[29]

These actions represent an appropriately balanced approach to a difficult issue. On the one hand, it is reasonable to encourage the development of efficient and effective clearing systems, which can reduce systemic risk. On the other hand, there is a need for a cautious, case-by-case evaluation of individual systems (which may, for example, concentrate risk in a centralised counterparty).

The final swaps exemption rules include two other very

26. Letter from William Wiles, Secretary to the Board of Governors of the Federal Reserve System, to Jean Webb, Secretary to the CFTC, regarding 17 CFR Part 35, Exemption for Certain Swap Agreements, p. 2 (28 Jan. 1993).

27. 58 Fed. Reg. 5587 at 5591.

28. Id.

29. Id.

important changes. In respect of those transactions that would otherwise be subject to CFTC jurisdiction, the rules retain the applicability of both the anti-fraud and the anti-manipulation provisions of the Commodity Exchange Act. These provisions will help to ensure that the exemption rules do not provide a shield for boiler room operators seeking a new venue for their scams or unscrupulous traders seeking to manipulate cash commodity or futures prices.

## 5. THE HYBRID INSTRUMENTS EXEMPTION

At the same time as it issued the swaps exemption, the Commission also adopted final rules for 'hybrid' instruments that combine equity or debt securities or depository interests with features of either commodity futures or option contracts, or both.[30]

Hybrids presented the Commission with a markedly different set of policy issues. With swaps, the question had been *whether* to regulate since, apart from the Commodity Exchange Act, there was arguably no system of federal financial regulation applicable to those instruments. Hybrids, however, were potentially subject to both banking and securities regulatory systems (in addition to CFTC regulation) and the question became, '*which* system should apply to *which* instrument'.

The Commission addressed this issue by devising a rather complex 'predominant purpose' test. The test decomposes a hybrid into its component parts and compares the price exposure associated with the 'commodity-dependent component' and the value of the 'commodity-independent component'. If the commodity-independent component predominates, the instrument is exempt from CFTC regulation. Since exempt instruments will be subject to other regulatory regimes, the Commission did not retain anti-fraud or anti-manipulation authority.

30. 58 Fed. Reg. 5580 (22 Jan. 1993).

# 6. THE ENERGY PRODUCTS EXEMPTION

The Commission's third use of its exemptive authority was taken in response to an application for relief filed by a group of producers, processors, merchandisers and other commercial participants in businesses involving crude oil, natural gas or their products. The Commission's Order exempted contracts for the deferred purchase or sale of specified energy products among 'commercial participants' who, among other things: 'incur risks, in addition to price risk, related to the underlying physical commodities'; who 'have a demonstrable capacity ... to make or take delivery'; and who fall within defined categories of 'appropriate persons'.[31]

This Order was approved on a split vote. I voted against it primarily because, unlike the swaps exemption, the Order failed to retain the applicability of the general anti-fraud provisions of the Commodity Exchange Act. In my view, the exemption is overbroad, extending well beyond the previous limits of the forward contract exclusion and potentially exempting boiler room fraud operations. The exemption employs a 'commerciality' requirement that is largely undefined. It relies on the 'sophistication' of market participants, ignoring the fact that sophisticated firms are also susceptible to fraud. I believe it sets a dangerous precedent for future uses of the Commission's exemptive authority. The Chairman of the CFTC's jurisdictional subcommittee in the House of Representatives subsequently introduced legislation that would, if passed, reinstate the Act's anti-fraud provisions with respect to these transactions.[32]

# 7. FUTURE CFTC ACTIONS

There are several critical issues relating to derivatives that the CFTC will have to deal with in the near future.

---

31. 58 Fed. Reg. 21286 at 21294 (20 Apr. 1993).
32. H.R. 2374, 103d Cong. 1st Sess. (1993).

## 7.1 Futures style clearing for OTC Derivatives

Various groups have discussed the potential need for some type of centralised clearing system, modelled after the futures exchange clearing houses, as a response to systemic risk in the OTC market. The greatest concern has focused on risks in the swaps market. E. Gerald Corrigan, President of the Federal Reserve Bank of New York, raised this issue in a much publicised January 1992 speech to the New York State Bankers Association. He warned that interest rate swaps could be introducing 'new elements of risk' into the marketplace, including 'possible distortions to the balance sheets and income statements of financial and non-financial institutions alike'.

A series of recent reports and studies have focused on the potential benefits of netting arrangements for OTC instruments. For example, in November 1990, the Bank for International Settlements (BIS) published the Lamfalussy Report. This concluded that netting schemes have the potential to reduce systemic risk in OTC derivatives, if certain conditions are met, and suggested a series of minimum standards for netting systems. More recently, in April 1993 (at the same time as it issued for comment a set of consultative papers dealing with capital requirements), the BIS requested comment on a proposal for the use of bilateral netting to expand the novation netting permitted in the current Basle Accord of 1988. In July 1993 the Group of Thirty (G30) Global Derivatives Study Group published its study entitled, 'Derivatives: Practices and Principles'. The G30 study suggested that derivatives users should reduce credit risk by broadening the use of multi-product master agreements with close-out netting arrangements and urged regulators and legislators to recognise close-out netting arrangements and amend the Basle Accord to reflect their benefits in bank capital regulations.

As noted above, the CFTC has also taken an interest in OTC clearing issues and the swaps exemption rules specifically state that the Commission would welcome proposals for a swaps clearing house. At a 5 August, 1993 meeting of the CFTC Financial Products Advisory Committee, which I chair, I asked a panel of industry and exchange experts to focus on some of the practical business issues that could be involved in the formation of a swaps clearing house.

While the most obvious function of a swaps clearing house would be to provide for the reduction of systemic risk through multilateral netting, the panelists noted a variety of other useful functions, including: providing the clearing house guarantee; data collection and trade matching; evaluating and pricing positions and calculating the exposure that results from them (offset); cash and collateral management; managing the risk of market participants; admission of new participants and discipline of existing ones; general management, operation and governance functions; and managing relations with regulators and bankers.

It was generally agreed that a swaps clearing house would provide a number of benefits. The amount of trading in the existing swaps market is severely constrained by counterparty credit risk. Even those with strong credit are experiencing liquidity gaps as the long duration of swap transactions soaks up counterparty credit lines. Existing bilateral netting arrangements impose a high cost of entry for new participants and high operational costs. Multilateral netting by novation through a clearing house would: reduce systemic risk by improving credit availability and liquidity; reduce operational costs; and potentially reduce capital charges, depending on the system's structure and its regulator.

On the other hand, the panel identified some very serious impediments to the development of a swaps clearing house. From a structural point of view, swaps are highly customized instruments with low trading volume (at least compared to futures) so that opportunities to offset are limited. Also, swaps are denominated in a wide variety of currencies. Because many big market makers are banks, a multinational swaps clearing house would have to deal with many different bank regulators. Furthermore, the greatest need for a clearing house would be among the least liquid currencies, which would be least welcome to the clearing house owners.

Furthermore, many swaps are options or have options embedded in them and doing risk management for options demands that the clearing house be able to measure volatility.

But there is neither a consensus provider of volatility information for swaps, nor any other good way to measure this volatility. Finally, the existing system of bilateral counterparty credit limits does work and untethering the swaps market from these self-imposed limits could have undesirable systemic risk implications.

The panelists also discussed competitive impediments to a swaps clearing house. Futures clearing organisations owe their status to a statutory monopoly that is not available to a swaps clearing house. Market participants will have to *give up* their existing practices to embrace a new clearing house system. The willingness to give up those existing practices, however, is a function of market position. Thus, it is the least creditworthy institutions that need a clearing house the most and would embrace it most eagerly. But the most credit-worthy – without whom it would be impossible to achieve the 'critical mass' to make the clearing system work – are indifferent at best, or even hostile, due to the fear of losing market power. Also, apart from the guarantee function, there are credible substitutes for every function of a swaps clearing house. As the functionality of these substitutes improves, the incremental need for a swaps clearing house diminishes. Finally, the start-up costs of a swaps clearing house would be tremendous.

Despite the real impediments to the development of more sophisticated clearing systems in OTC markets, I believe that, properly designed clearing systems would help both in reducing risk in those markets and in reducing the danger of 'flow-back' risk in the exchange markets the CFTC currently regulates. I hope that the Commission's invitation will stimulate further efforts toward the development of clearing houses for swaps and other OTC instruments.

## 7.2 Proposals for a two-tiered market structure

Another controversial issue facing the CFTC involves proposals that would have the effect of creating a two-tiered regulatory structure for futures markets. As noted above (notwithstanding a certain amount of potentially conflicting guidance), the legislative history of the CFTC's new general exemptive authority clearly contemplates that exchanges are equally eligible to apply for exemptive relief. On 16 August 1993, the Commission published for comment exemption applications from the two largest US futures exchanges.[33]

The Chicago Mercantile Exchange (CME) petition is limited to the 'Rolling Spot'[34] currency futures and options contracts which the Commission approved for trading earlier in 1993. The exchange, which expects this contract to be traded exclusively by 'sophisticated investors,' seeks an exemption from certain statutory and regulatory provisions aimed primarily at protecting retail customers. The list of 'Eligible Rolling Spot Participants' who may trade the contracts generally tracks the criteria for 'appropriate persons' set out in the Futures Trading Practices Act of 1992, but also includes 'any natural person with total assets exceeding at least $10,000,000' and 'an exchange member of the CME, trading on his or her own behalf or on behalf of another Eligible Rolling Spot Participant'.[35] The exchange does not seek an exemption from the anti-fraud or anti-manipulation provisions of the Act, nor from the minimum financial requirements for brokers.

The Chicago Board of Trade's much broader petition asks the Commission to draft rules establishing a 'professional trading market exemption.' The exemption would apply to 'professional traders' (essentially the same definition as 'Eligible Rolling Spot Participant') trading in any contract on any designated exchange. The exemption would extend to all provisions of the Act[36] and CFTC regulations, subject to certain conditions. Thus, the transactions still would have to be cleared through a 'Commission-approved mutualised-risk clearing system' and still be subject to anti-fraud and anti-

33. 58 Fed. Reg. 43414 (16 Aug. 1993).

34. A 'rolling spot' futures contract is designed to continuously reflect the spot price of a foreign currency relative to the US dollar. It is intended to provide participants in the existing OTC interbank foreign currency market with the benefits of an exchange-traded market (in terms of costs, price transparency and counterparty credit exposure).

35. 58 Fed. Reg. 43414 at 43415.

36. Except section 2(a)(1)(B), the CFTC/SEC jurisdictional accord.

manipulation rules (to be drafted by the Commission specifically for these transactions).

In effect, these petitions would create a two-tiered market with less restrictive rules for 'sophisticated investors' and professional traders than for retail customers. I supported publishing these petitions for comment as a way to facilitate a necessary debate and to create a public record. While the *Federal Register* document contains an exhaustive list of questions, I see three paramount issues concerning these exchange applications.

First, to what extent are the competitive challenges presented by OTC markets a function of regulatory requirements imposed on exchanges and to what extent are they merely a function of business considerations, such as the ability to obtain a customised product or execute a larger transaction in the OTC market?

Secondly, to the extent regulation does create competitive disadvantages, are they offset by regulatory benefits such as increased investor confidence in the financial integrity of the system or the ability to get best price execution?

Thirdly, the premise of both applications seems to be that regulatory safeguards are unnecessary where trading is confined to certain classes of so-called 'sophisticated investors'. I hope institutional customers will tell us whether this premise is correct. Is it really the case that they do not benefit from safeguards such as market surveillance, financial integrity requirements and trade practice rules? More fundamentally, if we adopt the approach the exchanges have proposed – given the dominance of institutions in today's futures markets – could a parallel public market continue to survive? If not, are there more incremental measures the Commission could take to enhance competitiveness while maintaining the integrity of the markets and the CEA's core regulatory structure?

## 8. PENDING CFTC REAUTHORISATION

Very shortly, the CFTC will once again face the ordeal of Congressional reauthorisation. The Futures Trading Practices

Act of 1992 extended the CFTC's authorisation for only two years, until 31 October 1994. One reason for this shortest reauthorization period in the agency's history is to give the Congress an opportunity to revisit the issue of derivative instruments with an eye toward additional legislative action. Indeed, the conference report on the FTPA specifically states that '... it would be useful in the development of legislation relating to markets for derivative financial products to acquire more extensive and specific information in their regard than is currently available'.[37] Thus, the CFTC is directed to conduct a comprehensive study of swaps and off-exchange derivatives trading to determine, among other things:

(1) the size, scope, activities, and potential risks presented by the markets for swaps and other off-exchange derivative financial products;
(2) the need for additional regulatory controls that should be applicable to the products described in paragraph (1); [and]
(3) how any such regulatory controls could be implemented in a cost effective manner.[38]

The Commission presented this report to the Congress on 28 October 1993. In addition to background materials, a glossary, a bibliography, interviews with market participants, and a survey of academic literature, the report included: an analysis of potential risks, both systemic (*eg*, 'meltdown') and market specific (*eg*, settlement risk); a brief summary of accounting and disclosure issues; a quantitative evaluation of the size and scope of the OTC derivatives market; and an overview of the existing regulatory structure, both domestically and internationally.

On 27 October 1993 the Commission hosted a day-long symposium entitled 'OTC Derivative Markets and their Regulation: The Report of the Commodity Futures Trading Commission'. Speakers representing the CFTC, other federal agencies, futures exchanges, OTC market participants and

37. H.R. Rep. 978 at 83.
38. Id.

academe discussed the report and the important derivative market issues it covers.

Congress also directed the CFTC to include in its study of swaps and off-exchange derivatives trading a review of the 'public policy implications' of two recent court decisions interpreting the Commodity Exchange Act. One case, *Kromenhoek v A-Mark Precious Metals*,[39] raises issues concerning the distinction between futures and forward contracts. While the CEA declares that a forward (which the Act specifically excludes from CFTC jurisdiction) is *not* a future, the *A-Mark* court declared the contract at issue to be *both* a forward *and* a future. While some have argued that this confusion over the breadth of the forwards exclusion could open a loophole for fraud, the Commission has maintained that the *A-Mark* decision does not affect its ability to protect the public from illegal off-exchange futures scams.

The other case which Congress directed the CFTC to study is *Tauber v Salomon Forex Inc., et. al.*[40] The Tauber case involves the breadth of the 'Treasury amendment,' the section of the CEA which provides that:

> Nothing in this Act shall be deemed to govern or in any way be applicable to transactions in foreign currency ... unless such transactions involve the sale thereof for future delivery conducted on a board of trade.[41]

The Commission's position is that the Treasury amendment is intended solely to exclude the interbank foreign currency market from CFTC jurisdiction. The agency argues that the *Tauber* court's overly broad interpretation – that all off-exchange foreign currency futures are excluded from CFTC jurisdiction – would open the door to fraudulent, off-exchange foreign currency boiler rooms. Indeed, one such boiler room operation, faced with a CFTC enforcement action, has already sought to use the *Tauber* decision as a shield. The court, however, rejected the defendant's argument

---

39. 945 F. 2nd 309 (9th Cir. 1991) (Also referred to as *In Re: Bybee*).
40. E.D. Va., 1 June 1992, Appeal Pending, Case No. 92–1406 (4th Cir.).
41. Commodity Exchange Act, section 2(a)(1)(A)(ii), 7 USC section 2(a)(1) (1974).

and accepted the Commission's interpretation of the Treasury amendment.[42] This sets up a potential conflict between Circuit Courts of Appeal, which might require a Supreme Court ruling to resolve.

The final ongoing issue facing the CFTC involves its own future as an independent agency with exclusive jurisdiction over futures markets. The Commission's last reauthorisation saw unsuccessful proposals to merge the CFTC with the Securities and Exchange Commission. More recently, Jack Sandner, the Chairman of the Chicago Mercantile Exchange, has proposed merging seven financial regulatory agencies, plus certain regulatory responsibilities of the Federal Reserve Board and the Labor Department, into a single cabinet level Federal Financial Regulatory Service.

Also, Congress has directed the Commission to study, as the final topic in the swaps and derivatives study ordered in the conference report on the FTPA, 'whether a single Federal regulatory agency should regulate the exchange or off-exchange trading of, and markets for, futures, options, swaps, derivative products, and securities'.[43]

# 9. CONCLUSION

Clearly, the US regulatory structure for derivative instruments, both on-exchange and off-exchange, will face considerable stresses and challenges over the next few years. Perhaps the greatest challenge for the CFTC will involve maintaining an appropriate balance between preventing the erosion of the competitiveness of regulated exchanges in the face of growing competition from OTC markets and preserving the core regulatory protections that form the heart of the Commodity Exchange Act.

42. *CFTC v Standard Forex, Inc., et. al.* CV-93-0088 (EDNY 9 Aug. 1993).
43. H.R. Rep. 978 at 83.

*Chapter 3*

# GROWTH AND SYSTEMIC RISKS IN DERIVATIVES MARKETS

Dr. Horst Bockelmann,
Economic Adviser, Bank for International
Settlements

## 1. INTRODUCTION

The explosive growth of the derivatives markets in the last decade has been one of the most spectacular developments in financial markets, not only in recent history but presumably by any standards. Much has been said and written with regard to both causes and effects. On the causes side, it would clearly not have happened without a strong and broadly based demand for instruments that facilitate hedging and position-taking, itself no doubt a result of the increased volatility in financial markets observed since the early 1970s. Also prominent on the causes side is the quantum leap in technology, which was a precondition for routinely applying mathematical artistry to the pricing of derivatives. I shall not pursue these aspects any further here. Among the effects I shall only mention, with a question mark: does the growth of derivatives business increase the potential for systemic disruptions in financial markets?

## 2. STATISTICS AND DATA COLLECTION

The two aspects 'growth' and 'systemic risks' are in fact quite closely related to each other. Questions about systemic risks arise only once the activities concerned have grown beyond a certain critical threshold. There is very little doubt that

33

derivatives business has indeed passed this point. But measuring the size of the market is no easy task. The official statistical coverage of banks' off-balance-sheet business, of which derivatives business represents the most important part, has been improved somewhat in several countries. However, significant gaps and differences between national reporting systems remain. Central banks have, furthermore, tended to limit their efforts to those dealers in financial derivatives that fall under their traditional 'jurisdiction' within the normal boundaries of the monetary and financial sectors, which omits a sizeable part of the market.

Private associations such as the International Swap Dealers Association have filled the void in respect of the over-the-counter markets in swap-related financial derivatives. This is a valuable service but, given its voluntary nature, it is not surprising that the reporting lags are long. Figures for outstanding amounts of interest rate and currency swaps at the end of 1992 were only released in autumn 1993. Statistics on derivative financial instruments traded on organised exchanges worldwide are available much more quickly, which again is not surprising since the exchanges themselves are the counterparty in each transaction and thus only have to add them up. However, comprehensive data on foreign exchange options, forward rate agreements and equity and commodity contracts are not available from any source.

Apart from deciding who should collect statistics on derivatives, there is the question as to what data should actually be collected. For over-the-counter interest rate and currency swaps notional amounts are normally the only data easily available. The notional principal amount for interest rate swaps provides the common basis for calculating the two interest streams to be swapped; but it is only a calculating device and it does not figure in any payment transactions, nor does it represent at any time a measure of possible credit exposure. For this reason notional principal amounts give an inflated picture of what is involved in interest rate swaps. In currency swaps the matter is only a little different: principal amounts may be exchanged or not, depending on the contract, but the amounts at risk (apart from settlement risks of the Herstatt type) depend on exchange rate

## Table 1 Markets for selected derivative financial instruments

Notional principal amounts outstanding at end-year, in billions of US dollars

| | 1986 | 1987 | 1988 | 1989 | 1990 | 1991 | 1992 |
|---|---|---|---|---|---|---|---|
| Exchange-traded instruments ........ | 589.0 | 727.3 | 1,304.6 | 1,767.5 | 2,290.5 | 3,519.7 | 4,783.3 |
| Interest rate futures................ | 370.0 | 487.7 | 895.4 | 1,200.7 | 1,454.2 | 2,157.1 | 3,048.2 |
| Interest rate options[1] | 146.5 | 121.8 | 279.2 | 387.9 | 599.5 | 1,072.6 | 1,385.4 |
| Currency futures..................... | 10.0 | 14.1 | 11.6 | 15.6 | 16.3 | 17.8 | 24.5 |
| Currency options[1] ................. | 39.2 | 59.5 | 48.0 | 50.1 | 55.7 | 59.5 | 80.0 |
| Stock market index futures........ | 14.9 | 18.1 | 27.8 | 41.8 | 69.7 | 77.3 | 81.3 |
| Options on stock market indices[1] | 8.4 | 26.1 | 42.7 | 71.5 | 95.2 | 135.5 | 163.9 |
| | | | | | | | |
| Over-the-counter-instruments[2] ..... | 500.0[e] | 866.6 | 1,329.8 | 2,425.1 | 3,450.3 | 4,449.5 | 5,345.7 |
| Interest rate swaps[3] .............. | 400.0[e] | 682.9 | 1,010.2 | 1,526.0 | 2,311.5 | 3,065.1 | 3,850.8 |
| Currency and cross-currency interest rate swaps[3,4] ................. | 100.0[e] | 183.7 | 319.6 | 449.1 | 577.5 | 807.2 | 860.4 |
| Other derivative instruments[3,4,5] | – | – | – | 450.0 | 561.3 | 577.2 | 634.5 |

e = estimate.

1. Calls plus puts.
2. No statistics are available on forward rate agreements or over-the-counter foreign exchange options. Only data collected by ISDA.
3. Contracts between ISDA members reported only once.
4. Adjusted for reporting of both currencies.
5. Caps, collars, floors and swaptions.

*Sources:* Futures Industry Association (FIA); various futures and options exchanges worldwide: International Swap Dealers Association (ISDA); BIS calculations.

movements in much the same way as interest rate swaps do on interest rate movements. For derivative financial instruments traded on organised exchanges an alternative measure is available: the annual turnover, in the form of numbers of standardised contracts traded.

Efforts towards improving the statistics on derivatives may be helped by better accounting and disclosure standards. In this context the US Financial Accounting Standards Board Interpretation No. 39, which takes effect in 1994, will put the current credit exposure of each swap dealer on to the balance sheet, based on the net market value of all transactions written under a single master agreement. Improvements to and some harmonisation of accounting practices may not be a prerequisite, but they will certainly enhance the chances of collecting meaningful statistics.

It is no doubt easier to use the word 'meaningful' than to convey a clear idea of what is actually meaningful with regard to derivatives and what is not. Criticising notional principal amounts as giving an inflated picture, because – at least with regard to interest rate swaps – there are no corresponding (principal) cash flows or credit exposures involved, suggests looking for measures of cash flows arising from derivatives, either in the form of up-front compensation for assuming a risk (such as an option premium) or in the form of settlement payments as a result of movements in interest or exchange rates or in equity or commodity prices. To the extent that derivatives transactions generate payment obligations they result in credit exposures.

Measures of this kind, if they became available in sufficient detail, would represent a major step forward. But even they would not give the whole story. Derivatives transfer or exchange certain risks between two parties. Cash payments and credit exposures – apart from fees and the spreads agreed in advance – measure the outcome of these transfers on the basis of hindsight rather than the risks that were originally exchanged. The same is true of marking to market on a daily or even on a real-time basis. These measures convey no information about the market risk exposure embedded in a derivatives book. The idea is gaining wider acceptance that the value-at-risk in a given derivatives portfolio should be

## Table 2 Derivative financial instruments traded on organised exchanges worldwide

Annual turnover, in millions of contracts

| | 1987 | 1988 | 1989 | 1990 | 1991 | 1992 |
|---|---|---|---|---|---|---|
| Interest rate futures | 145.7 | 156.3 | 201.0 | 219.1 | 234.7 | 335.4 |
| On short-term instruments | 29.4 | 33.7 | 70.2 | 75.8 | 84.8 | 130.8 |
| of which: three-month Euro-dollar rates[1] | 23.7 | 25.2 | 46.8 | 39.4 | 41.7 | 66.9 |
| three-month Euro-yen rates[2] | 0.0 | 0.0 | 4.7 | 15.2 | 16.2 | 17.4 |
| three-month Euro-DM rates[3] | 0.0 | 0.0 | 1.6 | 3.1 | 4.8 | 12.2 |
| On long-term instruments | 116.3 | 122.6 | 130.8 | 143.3 | 149.9 | 204.6 |
| of which: US Treasury bonds[4] | 69.4 | 73.8 | 72.8 | 78.2 | 69.9 | 71.7 |
| French government bonds[5] | 11.9 | 12.4 | 15.0 | 16.0 | 21.1 | 31.1 |
| Japanese government bonds[6] | 18.4 | 18.8 | 19.1 | 16.4 | 12.9 | 12.1 |
| German government bonds[7] | 0.0 | 0.3 | 5.3 | 9.6 | 12.4 | 18.9 |
| Interest rate options and options on interest rate futures | 29.3 | 30.5 | 39.5 | 52.0 | 50.8 | 64.8 |
| Currency futures | 20.8 | 22.1 | 27.5 | 29.1 | 29.2 | 30.7 |
| Currency options and options on currency futures | 18.2 | 18.2 | 30.7 | 18.8 | 21.5 | 23.0 |
| Total | 214.0 | 227.1 | 288.6 | 319.1 | 336.2 | 453.9 |
| of which: in the United States | 161.4 | 165.3 | 198.1 | 205.7 | 199.7 | 238.7 |
| in Europe | 27.2 | 32.6 | 49.0 | 61.0 | 84.4 | 140.5 |
| in Japan | 18.3 | 18.8 | 23.7 | 33.6; | 30.0 | 28.7 |

1. Traded on the Chicago Mercantile Exchange – International Monetary Market (CME-IMM), Singapore Mercantile Exchange (SIMEX), London International Financial Futures Exchange (LIFFE), Tokyo International Financial Futures Exchange (TIFFE) and Sydney Futures Exchange (SFE).
2. Traded on the TIFFE and SIMEX.
3. Traded on the Marché à Terme International de France (MATIF) and LIFE.
4. Traded on the Chicago Board of TRADE (CBOT), LIFFE, Mid-America Commodity Exchange (MIDAM), New York Futures Exchange (NYFE) and Tokyo Stock Exchange (TSE).
5. Traded on the MATIF.
6. Traded on the TSE, LIFFE and CBOT.
7. Traded on the LIFFE and Deutsche Terminbörse.
*Sources:* Futures Industry Association, various futures and options exchanges worldwide and BIS calculations.

ascertained not only daily under normal conditions (to compare it with market risk limits) but also in regular stress tests. The Group of Thirty includes this recommendation among the 25 recommendations in its recent study on derivatives published in July 1993. Such tests, once they have become common practice among major participants, could perhaps be used also to collect aggregate data for statistical purposes and for systemic risk monitoring.

But I am moving far ahead of present data availability. With regard to an idea of the phenomenal growth of the derivatives business, this can be gained from the data we have, even though they are not well suited for cross-market comparisons. In terms of the underlying notional principal amounts the new contracts for interest rate swaps struck over-the-counter in 1992 amounted to US$2.8 trillion, a 13-digit figure, and 74 per cent more than in 1991. This was the highest growth rate recorded since these statistics started to be collected in 1987. Growth rates of just under or just over 50 per cent were the order of the day from 1988 through 1990, but growth had come down to 'only' 28 per cent in 1991. If that was regarded of something as a 'maturing' of the interest rate swap market, the figures for 1992 seem to tell otherwise. However, in terms of amounts outstanding the picture differs quite significantly. The total amount outstanding was US$3.8 trillion at the end of 1992, roughly a quarter more than a year earlier. The large difference between the growth rates for flows and stocks reflects mainly a shift towards shorter original maturities among the newly arranged interest rate swap deals and the maturing of longer-dated contracts written in earlier years.

## 3. GROWTH

The difference between growth of flows and stocks is also striking for interest rate related swap derivatives, such as caps, floors, collars and swaptions. New contracts arranged in 1992 amounted to US$593 billion, an increase of 54.8 per cent over 1991. Stocks outstanding increased by only 10 per cent, to US$634 billion, however. In the case of currency swaps, new contracts of US$302 billion in 1992 actually represented a decrease by 8 per cent compared to 1991, while stocks increased by 6.6 per cent to US$860 billion. This reverse stock-flow pattern reflected in all probability the effect of exchange rate changes, for which these figures are not adjusted. The currency swap figures quoted seem to indicate that the currency swaps market is much smaller than the interest rate swaps market, but one should recall that notional principal amounts are a more distorting measure for interest rate swaps than for currency swaps, where principal amounts may actually be exchanged.

Tables 1–6 give the details, also regarding currency breakdown and the development of trading on organised exchanges worldwide, which grew by 36 per cent in 1992. Something is going on in these markets for which, at least in the major areas, the term 'explosive growth' is no exaggeration.

The word 'explosive' has of course unhappy connotations. It suggests destructive forces at work. What could go wrong in these markets? And could it have repercussions on other financial markets? Notes of warning have been sounded on several sides. They have been belittled by remarks such as 'Regulators are paid to worry'. But, looking at financial markets in general, the truth of the matter is that too many things have already gone wrong in a number of countries in the last 10–15 years and not just at the fringes of the industry. If they have not resulted in a full-fledged systemic crisis, that may have been due in part to good luck and to the extraordinary efforts of some unusually able people. Any presumption that large institutions will invariably have the expertise and wisdom needed to steer clear of disaster has been exposed as an illusion. Reference has been made in this context to 'Murphy's Law': what can go wrong, will go wrong. One might counter such fatalism by arguing that if disaster strikes it rarely comes from the generally expected direction. Could not the very worries about systemic dangers inherent in the explosive growth of derivatives business compel market participants to revamp their risk management policies and tighten internal controls against fraud and negligence to such a degree as to avoid what some fear? Presumably they could.

Still, I find it difficult to subscribe to such an optimistic view, at least as long as the over-the-counter market continues to grow in the way it has hitherto. Market participants often argue that the risks inherent in derivatives business, such as credit, market and liquidity risks, are no different from those encountered and managed by financial institutions in connection with their traditional business. Moreover, derivatives allow end-users to diversify or hedge risks they already carry, thus reducing their risk exposure overall and not increasing it.

The latter argument, of course, does not apply to those who act as intermediaries and market-makers or use derivatives to take positions. In many of these firms significant gaps remain at present between the desired risk management system and the system and capability actually in place. Centralised risk monitoring requires large investment in hardware and software which many firms cannot afford or are not prepared to undertake in the near future. The integrated management of derivatives portfolios, with a view to exploiting internal position offsets and thereby reducing capital and hedging costs, is far from being a reality in most firms. This does not stop them from attempting to exploit gains from correlations among prices in underlying markets or of exposures in individual product categories.

## 4. OTC TRADING

The growth of over-the-counter interbank trading in longer maturities contracts has made credit risk exposures a by-product of market risk trading activities to a much greater extent than in the past. Furthermore, trading in the over-the-counter market brings participants into contact, directly or indirectly, with other counterparties with which they have no long-term customer relationship and of whose exposures to various risks they know very little. The lack of transparency of balance sheets, and especially of what is omitted from

## Table 3 Markets for selected derivative instruments traded over-the-counter[1]
New contracts arranged, in billions of US dollars

| | 1987 | 1988 | 1989 | 1990 | 1991 | 1992 | Amounts outstanding at end 1992 |
|---|---|---|---|---|---|---|---|
| Interest rate swaps............... | 387.8 | 568.1 | 833.5 | 1,264.3 | 1,621.8 | 2,822.6 | 3,850.8 |
| Currency swaps[2] ..................... | 86.5 | 124.3 | 178.2 | 212.8 | 328.4 | 301.9 | 860.4 |
| Other swap-related derivatives[3] ... | – | – | 335.5 | 292.3 | 382.7 | 592.5 | 634.5 |
| Total[4] ............... | – | – | 1,347.2 | 1,769.3 | 2,332.9 | 3,717.0 | 5,345.7 |

1. Underlying notional principal amounts on which contracts are struck.
2. Adjusted for reporting of both sides, including cross-currency interest swaps.
3. Caps, collars, floors and swaptions.
4. Excluding other over-the-counter instruments such as forward rate agreements, currency options, forward foreign exchange transactions and equity and commodity-related derivatives, for which no statistics are available.
*Source:* ISDA.

them, is widely recognised as having greatly complicated the assessment and management of credit risk. There are also basic operational risks, in that a firm may mistakenly believe risks to be hedged when they are not, or participants may simply overestimate the liquidity of their own position owing to a false perception of their own share of transactions or positions in various markets. Some participants find it difficult to manage the cash requirements connected with large derivatives portfolios. Such cash requirements can arise suddenly and in large amounts when changes in market conditions or in perceptions of credit standing necessitate margin payments or the adjustment of hedges and positions.

## 5. DEFICIENCIES IN RISK MANAGEMENT PROCEDURES

Often, worries about deficiencies in risk management procedures focus on concerns that less experienced institutions are trying to get into what they perceive as a highly profitable market. But equally serious concerns arise from the high concentration of derivatives activity among a few large banks, which has not changed during the period when the markets have been expanding so rapidly. The derivatives portfolios of these banks are accounting for an ever greater proportion of the total business they undertake. From a systemic point of view, one cannot fail to notice that whatever risk there is must be rather unevenly spread, even though these institutions can generally be expected to be by far the most highly rated, the largest, the most sophisticated and the most risk-conscious institutions with presumably excellent managements.

The high concentration of derivatives business on not more than 50 institutions worldwide, with the bulk accounted for by a much smaller number and a heavy bias towards the United States, is not only worrying if one thinks of the systemic implications of the sudden failure of a major market participant, especially if it were to happen in an already unsettled market environment. It also gives cause for concern

# Table 4 Main features of the interest rate swap market
Notional principal value in billions of US dollars

| | US$ | Japanese yen | Deutsch mark | Pound sterling | Swiss franc | French franc | Other |
|---|---|---|---|---|---|---|---|
| **Swaps outstanding at end-1992** | | | | | | | |
| by counterparty: End-users...... | 906.3 | 264.7 | 168.8 | 157.6 | 70.0 | 101.8 | 300.8 |
| Interbank[1] .... | 853.9 | 441.3 | 175.6 | 137.2 | 70.4 | 37.3 | 165.0 |
| **New swaps in 1992** | | | | | | | |
| by counterparty: End-users...... | 688.7 | 165.8 | 109.6 | 106.2 | 36.8 | 177.5 | 201.7 |
| Interbank[1] .... | 647.1 | 261.8 | 127.6 | 100.0 | 43.5 | 31.8 | 124.6 |

1. Swaps between ISDA members adjusted for double-counting of positions.

*Source:* ISDA.

from the point of view of the way in which the decisions of certain players can affect particular markets. One does not have to think primarily of the danger of manipulation. The decisions can be taken in good faith. A firm active in the market may, in the event of a sharp market movement or other surprises, take the precaution of temporarily withdrawing from trading and from extending credit to counterparties which have come under suspicion.

Such a move may be enough to dry up liquidity in a particular market. But as the same players are active in different market segments, the likelihood is that the effects of such a withdrawal will quickly spread to other markets, on which other participants rely to adjust or close positions at a time of their choosing. This might apply above all to options, which, in the absence of a fully offsetting back-to-back option hedge, require dynamic hedging of underlying price exposures and – more complicated – hedging of volatility exposure. For these purposes options writers depend heavily on liquid and orderly cash, exchange-traded and over-the-counter options markets. It was not surprising that this was the area in which problems surfaced quickly at the time of the exchange market turbulence in the autumn of 1992, when volatility not only of exchange rates but also of short-term interest rates far exceeded what had been considered likely in worst-case scenarios and which had therefore been built into hedging programmes.

Nobody can claim that what we observe in this field are all robust and solid markets. There are markets with a large volume of transactions and with instruments at the low end of the risk spectrum, where the number of players is very large and brokers remain active. This is true of the market for forward rate agreements and short-term interest rate swaps. In markets where the degree of concentration is fairly high, I see potential systemic problems even though the individual institutions may be well-run and up to their task.

Systemic risk and the danger of a systemic crisis may have a somewhat academic ring to many market participants. Have not a number of governments let it be known that they would always step in if the integrity of their financial system were at stake? Other governments have not actually said so,

## Table 5 Composition of new currency swaps in 1992
In billions of US dollars

| | Total notional amount[2,3] | of which[1] | | of which | |
|---|---|---|---|---|---|
| | | Against US$[3] | Against other currencies[3] | End-user | Fixed/floating[3] |
| Japanese yen .................. | 72.3 | 50.0 | 22.3 | 51.3 | 29.7 |
| Swiss franc.................... | 42.8 | 16.8 | 26.0 | 34.8 | 17.2 |
| Deutschmark................. | 50.5 | 21.6 | 29.0 | 41.0 | 19.3 |
| ECU ............................ | 29.7 | 15.5 | 14.2 | 23.7 | 12.9 |
| Canadian dollar ............ | 34.3 | 30.5 | 3.9 | 31.9 | 14.0 |
| Pound sterling .............. | 30.9 | 17.0 | 13.9 | 26.6 | 9.7 |
| Italian lira.................... | 26.5 | 15.6 | 10.9 | 20.2 | 11.6 |
| Sub-total ..................... | 287.0 | 166.9 | 120.1 | 229.5 | 114.3 |
| Other .......................... | 104.5 | 45.3 | 59.2 | 76.2 | 61.5 |
| minus double counting of non-dollar swaps.................... | −89.7 | | −89.7 | −70.1 | −32.9 |
| Total........................... | 301.9 | 212.2 | 89.7 | 235.6 | 142.9 |

1. Provisional figures subject to revision.
2. Underlying notional principal amounts on which contracts are struck.
3. Adjusted for double-counting of positions reported by ISDA members.

*Source:* ISDA.

but have acted accordingly whenever the situation has arisen.

To take this view and to conclude that there is no reason to worry about systemic risk would, however, be rather short-sighted. It is true that governments arc prone to become involved in managing financial distress when it reaches a certain order of magnitude, notwithstanding the moral hazard this implies. The fact that governments are likely to step in at a certain stage does not, however, make a systemic crisis a harmless affair. Firstly, government involvement can itself be rather costly in more senses than one. It can also present serious technical problems. Unravelling a large derivatives portfolio of a firm in trouble can become a nightmare, particularly when in addition the firm's legal structure is highly diversified. Some daunting experience of this kind already exists. Secondly, if the crisis has an international dimension, it may require co-ordination among the authorities of different countries, which may be much more difficult to arrange than crisis management in a purely national context. Thirdly, even a well-contained systemic crisis can have repercussions on the real economy that may be more severe and last longer than anticipated. One only has to look at those countries that have experienced financial distress recently to see all this quite clearly.

To quote from our latest Annual Report, 'the costs of resolving financial distress put a premium on prevention'. The Promisel Report advocated efforts at three levels with a view to lessening the risks and strengthening safeguards to prevent local problems from developing into systemic threats: first, the improvement of risk management practices at the level of the individual firm; secondly, the improvement of the structural and institutional basis for certain wholesale activities at a collective level, comprising not only market participants, perhaps acting in concert, but also the legal, supervisory and regulatory authorities; and thirdly the improvement of transparency, not just in terms of enhanced disclosure by firms and improved statistical coverage but in terms of understanding which concepts would be of greatest relevance from the systemic risk perspective and which data would best fit those concepts. Equally important are the general responsibilities of central banks, which include understanding the roles and behaviour of firms operating in financial markets and how their own policy actions affect the environment in which these markets operate. One basic tenet of supervision is to ensure that banks and other financial institutions are adequately capitalised. Recently proposed capital requirements for market risk at banks will ensure that risks are better covered and costed. They will, however, not come into effect for another couple of years.

The recommendations of the report of G30 go basically in the same direction, although the report tends to play down not only the risks that will exist as long as these recommendations have not been implemented across the board but also the risks that will remain even after they have. Supervisors and regulators cannot afford to sit back and relax, nor can or should the principal participants active in these markets.

## Table 6 Main features of markets for swap-related derivative products
Notional principal amounts outstanding at end-year, in billions of US dollars

| | | 1990 | 1991 | 1992 |
|---|---|---|---|---|
| US dollar | Caps | 251.2 | 225.2 | 231.9 |
| | Floors | 75.9 | 73.2 | 62.2 |
| | Collars and other combinations | 32.7 | 12.6 | 13.7 |
| | Swaptions | 63.1 | 56.6 | 31.3 |
| | Total | 422.8 | 367.5 | 339.2 |
| Other currencies | Caps | 68.2 | 91.8 | 104.9 |
| | Floors | 34.2 | 56.0 | 76.6 |
| | Collars and other combinations | 4.9 | 9.5 | 17.9 |
| | Swaptions | 31.1 | 52.4 | 95.9 |
| | Total | 138.4 | 209.7 | 295.3 |
| All currencies | Caps | 319.4 | 317.0 | 336.8 |
| | Floors | 110.1 | 129.2 | 138.8 |
| | Collars and other combinations | 37.6 | 22.0 | 31.7 |
| | Swaptions | 94.2 | 109.0 | 127.2 |
| | Total | 561.3 | 577.2 | 634.5 |

*Source:* ISDA.

*Chapter 4*

# INTERNATIONAL REGULATION OF DERIVATIVES

Richard Farrant,
Chief Executive, Securities and Futures
Authority

## 1. INTRODUCTION

Why is it that derivatives, which have been around for
centuries, have so quickly become the flavour of the last two
years? To put it another way, why was it that New York
Federal Reserve Bank president Gerald Corrigan's warning in
January 1992 in a speech to New York bankers – itself only
one part of a broad survey of the state of US finance –
triggered off such a wave of introspection?

The simple answer is that he said what many people were
thinking; or rather feeling. I make that qualification
advisedly. Corrigan's remarks were not a reasoned argument; they were an expression of unease. As such, they struck
a chord in many others. Since then much debate, and still
more paper, has been devoted to explaining why so many
people feel uneasy. Happily the debate has not stood still;
indeed it has moved on rather fast. The Promisel report,
published by the Bank for International Settlements (BIS) in
1992, identified a number of reasons for concern, but
suggested few responses. The Group of Thirty report,
published in summer 1993, was designedly less analytic and
more practical.

# 2. KEY ISSUES

## 2.1 Necessary skills and techniques

Derivatives, like any attractive new technical gizmo, require new skills and analytic techniques which are initially in short supply. So long as the skills command a premium price, the profits from having them will be very attractive. That in turn will tempt those without the required infrastructure and skills into threatening and dangerous territory. The supervisor is trying to ensure that the attractions of the premium price do not obscure perception of the dangers.

The most important thing is to have recognised that it is not derivatives as such that have inherent deficiencies, but the shortage of skills necessary to use them sensibly. This is a temporary phenomenon, but no less worrying so long as it persists. For the supervisor there are two aspects to this. It is of some concern that there is so large a knowledge gap between a dozen or so key players of great skill and experience and the rest of the market. That could provide the opportunity for anti-competitive exploitation, although I know of no evidence at all for that. More to the point, the system is highly dependent on these key players, which is both a strength and a potential weakness. If one of them faltered, the ramifications for the rest of the market would be very considerable.

The other aspect of concern is that banks without the necessary skills may believe they can be acquired on the cheap. Although everyone pays lip service to the need to surround the dealers with pricing, confirmations, settlement, risk and liquidity control, legal and accounting systems, practices and expertise, all properly managed from above, it can too often be no more than lip service. The result is a lopsided skills base, which is probably worse than none at all, in that it breeds the illusion that there is something there of value. If there is one feature that distinguishes the key players from the rest it is their strength in every department. It is genuinely a case of the strength of the whole being no more than that of its weakest component.

Active participation by a bank in derivatives has so far proved to be – in the jargon – a high sunk costs game. It is necessary to spend a lot of money just to get started properly, and to recoup that high expenditure requires a level of income which is unlikely to be achieved quickly. One supervisory response, and some have been tempted to respond in this way, is to ban banks from even trying. The alternative is to tolerate cross-subsidy. Either a bank spends all the money required to start properly, cross-subsidised from the income generated by other activities, or it skimps on the full system and accepts that the higher risk of loss that results will be financed from other profit streams. It all sounds most unworthy of supervisory approval, but frankly there is no other way of improving the industry's skills base at the speed expected by customers of banks demanding better overall standards of service more cheaply. The supervisor must be convinced that there is sufficient scope for cross-subsidy, and that the risks from derivatives cannot overwhelm the capacity of the rest of the business to absorb them.

## 2.2 Securitisation

The second issue is securitisation. The flow of finance increasingly takes place through market trading rather than between an individual relationship between borrower and lender. I describe this broadly as securitisation. In my view, market trading has actually been more challenging to the banks than have derivatives *per se*, and much of the supervisory concern laid at the door of derivatives has more to do with banks' capabilities to conduct market trading safely.

In the recent debate on their safety, the defenders of derivatives have specially emphasised two characteristics, both of which are indisputable, but have not provided much effective defence. The first is that they are not new. That has cut little ice given the enormous growth of the market. They may not be new, but they have acquired a new dimension of significance. The second is that they are used defensively to protect or close out a financial position as much, if not more, than they are used speculatively, to create one. Derivatives' defenders have often seemed puzzled why this also has cut little ice. There is a simple answer. The principal concern has been less about the intrinsic merits of derivatives; and more about the potential impact of securitisation generally on individual banks and the banking system as a whole.

For banks and for bank supervisors, securitisation has been as much as anything a cultural issue; witness the huge efforts and expense required by the UK clearing banks to come to terms with new trading operations following the opening up of the London Stock Exchange in 1986. Traditional banking involved a network of bilateral relationships with customers, transacting contracts such as loans that could not be instantly valued. Securitisation involves multilateral relationships through 'the market', and that involves transacting contracts which have a market price and can be instantly valued. A complete change of style, personality and pace is necessary. Now that the clearers have broadly met that challenge it is easy to forget how large it was. But it has yet to work fully through the banking system, particularly abroad.

## 2.3 Over-the-counter markets

The third issue is the rise to new prominence of over-the-counter (OTC) markets. Demand for tailor-made derivatives have enormously promoted trading over the counter, rather than through an organised exchange. Over-the-counter trading was likely to increase anyway, as information technology improved alternative means of communication to the traditional central trading floor. But derivatives facilitate the tailor-making of a financial instrument to meet a particular need, and OTC trading is much more tolerant of non-standard contracts, than trading through an exchange.

The lack of structure of OTC markets can be a source of real concern to supervisors and central banks. The lack of standardisation of contract, terms of dealing, confirmations, or procedures for settlement and payment broaden the area of risk for each participant and range of skills needed to deal with them. One consequence is that lawyers have a bonanza!

There is no central authority well placed to monitor statistical and other indicators of market trends and to react pre-emptively by, for example, raising margin requirements when unhealthy tendencies are detected. Everything depends on the recognition by market players of a sense of responsibility for the well-being of the market as a whole. Successful solutions to market problems depend on the co-operation of counter-parties. As the market broadens, will it always work so well? If not, what will happen?

## 3. SUPERVISORY ISSUES

Combining these different developments – derivatives, securitisation, and the rise of OTC trading – itself generates a number of supervisory issues.

Firstly, derivatives have introduced much longer-term exposure of one counterparty to the capability of the other to perform his side of the contract than was common before in trading markets. The extension of 'credit' risk this has caused has been compounded by the need to enter new deals to control market positions. The result is a potentially destabilising mushrooming of credit risks. That needs to be safely collapsed and the obvious way to do this is by ensuring that legally robust netting arrangements are in place.

Secondly, the valuation of derivatives is complex and by its nature uncertain, depending on mathematical techniques that are still evolving and on assumptions that, if ever valid, may cease to be as life moves on. This mixes with the quick but unpredictable response of traded markets to new facts or new fears, and the opacity of OTC markets, into a cocktail with high potential instability. The interaction between derivative and underlying markets is not yet well enough understood to feel confident it might not be troublesome; nor is the capacity for derivatives to link several markets together.

Thirdly, the migration of financial intermediation from banking to traded markets challenges the institutional arrangements to deal with the threat of systemic break-down. It is less clear that banks remain the core of the system, and that central banks should continue to focus their surveillance and potential protection narrowly on them. But where are the boundaries to be drawn?

## 4. CONCLUSION

It would be all too easy at this point to conclude by repeating Corrigan's warning to his New York bankers to which I referred in the Introduction. But that would diminish the considerable progress in the period since he spoke. In that period, bank supervisors in all the G10 countries have concluded that derivatives are not only here to stay, but that they are a considerable force for good. Whether we like it or not, interest and exchange rates, share, commodity and other asset prices are unlikely to become less volatile, while banks are under ever more intense competitive pressure to operate with the slenderest safety margins. If interest margins are 5 per cent, a failure to protect against changes in interest rates is unlikely to do more than diminish a positive return. If margins are one tenth of that, much more is at stake. Derivatives have become a vital tool to manage these risks more precisely, and to enable the safety margins to be reduced. Naturally the regulators have wished to place a prudent limit to the process; hence their drive to agree minimum capital requirements.

Where will it all lead in terms of regulation? First on my agenda is to seek to ensure that each supervisor has the means to make an accurate assessment of the skills applied to the business of the significant derivatives players under his wing. That is not a matter for international harmonisation; it is a call to make sure that the supervisors themselves are equipped to do their routine job. It is easy to overlook the fact that supervisors face just as great a challenge in keeping up with change as does the market.

My second suggested priority is supervisory recognition of netting. This is easy to say, but less easy to do, given the combination of an international market operating under national law. But it is a real priority; the credit mushroom is the most obviously unstable and unnecessary element in the field of derivatives.

My third priority is more assurance that all the major players are subject to comprehensive supervisory overview. The principle of consolidated supervision is well established for banks, but much less firmly for securities houses.

Fourth is better statistical coverage of OTC markets. It is disturbing that so little facts are known and, in the absence of facts, assumptions have to be made which could become dangerously unreal.

Fifth, the regulators should encourage as much standardisation of procedures and agreements in OTC markets as can be realistically delivered. An element of anarchy is inherent in OTC and the capacity to innovate which this permits is an essential part of their appeal. But predictability of documentation and settlement is a great safeguard and, as derivative markets mature, more common elements can be identified and standardised, including disclosure standards. The development of master agreements is an obvious example, and there are very few who would argue they have been a bad idea.

I am assuming in all this that something sensible will come out of the present consultation on minimum capital requirements for market-related risks by the Basle Supervisors' Committee, and that the EC Capital Adequacy Directive will be fully implemented. I have heard complaints that these are unnecessarily complex. It is certainly true that the supervisory need could be met by a much simpler framework than those which have been proposed. But a simpler measure would require a higher safety margin of capital cover, and that is unlikely to be accepted by all banks.

In a nutshell, the role of international regulation at this stage is, in my view, really rather limited. What is most needed is good national regulation; that is challenge enough. I repeat that the new skills needed for derivatives are as much, if not more, of a challenge for the supervisors than for the banks. Implementing the international initiatives now on the table will already absorb much of the available expertise. A very high burden of proof of need is required to justify any more just now.

*Chapter 5*

# PROSPECTS FOR ASSET CONTINGENT VALUATION MODELS IN PRICING AND CREDIT RISK ASSESSMENT

## Kenneth D. Garbade,
## Managing Director, Bankers Trust Company

1993 marks the twentieth anniversary of the remarkable article[1] by Fischer Black and Myron Scholes on 'The Pricing of Options and Corporate Liabilities'. The enormous literature spawned by that article has focused primarily on the first part of the authors' interests – pricing conventional put and call options on common stock. Pricing corporate liabilities is not exactly a backwater, but it has certainly received much less attention. It is also the topic of my recent research and my comments here.

## 1. THE BASIC CONCEPT

Simply stated, the principle concept is a matter of viewing the assemblage of all of a corporation's assets as an underlying asset (analogous to common stock in the conventional call option pricing model) on which a variety of contingent claims, or derivative instruments, are written to finance the enterprise. The claims are contingent in the sense that their values depend, *inter alia*, on the current and prospective future values of the firm's assets.

Consider, for example, the simplest case examined by

---

1. Fischer Black and Myron Scholes, 'The Pricing of Options and Corporate Liabilities', *Journal of Political Economy*, 81 (1973), pp. 637–54.

Merton.[2] A firm is capitalised with (a) common stock paying no dividend and (b) a finite maturity zero coupon bond with aggregate face value F. If the firm's assets are worth more than F at the maturity of the bond the bondholders receive F and the stockholders receive the residual. If the assets are worth less than F the bondholders get the assets and the stockholders get nothing – an outcome familiarly known as bankruptcy. Thus, the common stock has the attributes of a call option on the assets of the firm with exercise price F and an expiration date equal to the maturity date of the debt. The bondholders are 'long' the assets of the firm and 'short' the call option held by the stockholders. Valuing the stock and debt at dates prior to the maturity of the debt follows by analogy with call option pricing.

This perspective on the valuation of corporate securities has been extended to coupon-bearing debt,[3] senior and subordinated debt,[4] convertible bonds,[5] callable bonds[6], bonds with market purchase option sinking funds,[7] and warrants.[8] It has also been used to examine the purposes and functions of a wide variety of debt covenants.[9]

2. Robert Merton, 'On the Pricing of Corporate Debt: The Risk Structure of Interest Rates', *Journal of Finance*, 29 (1974), pp. 449–70.

3. Michael Brennan and Eduardo Schwartz, 'Convertible Bonds: Valuation and Optimal Strategies for Call and Conversion', *Journal of Finance*, 32 (1977), pp. 1699–715.

4. Fischer Black and John Cox, 'Valuing Corporate Securities: Some Effects of Bond Indenture Provisions', *Journal of Finance*, 31 (1976), pp. 351–67.

5. See footnote 3 and Jonathan Ingersoll, 'A Contingent-Claims Valuation of Convertible Securities', *Journal of Financial Economics*, 4 (1977), pp. 289–322.

6. Michael Brennan and Eduardo Schwartz, 'Analyzing Convertible Bonds', *Journal of Financial and Quantitative Analysis*, 15 (1980), pp. 907–929.

7. Thomas Ho and Ronald Singer, 'The Value of Corporate Debt with a Sinking-Fund Provision', *Journal of Business*, 57 (1984), pp. 315–36.

8. Dan Galai and Meir Schneller, 'Pricing of Warrants and the Value of the Firm', *Journal of Finance*, 33 (Dec. 1978), pp. 1333–42.

9. See footnote 4 and Clifford Smith and Jerold Warner, 'On Financial Contracting', *Journal of Financial Economics*, 7 (1979), pp. 117–61.

# 2. APPLICATIONS

Asset contingent valuation of corporate securities has two significant applications at an institution such as Bankers Trust, which is in the business of purchasing, selling, and underwriting corporate securities as well as lending to corporations.

First, it can provide guidance in estimating the values of different classes of debt and equity and hence provide benchmarks for pricing new corporate claims. Similarly, it can help identify relatively overvalued and undervalued securities issued by a single firm and thus guide arbitrage transactions and/or reallocations of existing loan and investment portfolios to cure such mispricing.

Second, it can provide guidance in assessing the concentration and diversification of credit risks in a loan or bond portfolio. Commercial bankers are typically quite interested in whether their loan portfolios are excessively concentrated in a small number of closely related industries or whether they are well diversified across a large number of more unrelated industries. This issue cannot be resolved simply by examining the business activities of the respective borrowers and the face amounts of their loans. *Ceteris paribus,* a loan to a more highly leveraged company implies greater exposure to the risk of adverse fluctuations in the asset value of the firm and hence greater exposure to the businesses in which the firm is engaged. Credit risk assessment requires a capital structure model which reflects how underlying industry risks pass through to creditors on a loan-by-loan and firm-by-firm basis, so that the resulting exposures of the loan portfolio as a whole to the underlying industry risks can be calculated.

# 3. PROBLEMS

In view of the significance of the foregoing applications it is somewhat surprising that relatively little use has been made of asset contingent valuation of corporate securities. This is even more remarkable when we consider the widespread application of contingent claims analysis to derivative instruments such as conventional put and call options and interest rate caps, floors, and collars.

I believe there are two primary difficulties with applying contingent claims analysis to corporate securities: (a) specifying the partial differential equation which relates the dynamic evolution of the value of a claim to the evolution of the value of the corporation's assets, and (b) specifying the boundary conditions for the value of the claim.

## 3.1 Specifying the partial differential equation

One practical problem with specifying the partial differential equation is illustrated in Merton's 1974 analysis.[10] He assumes the firm makes dividend and interest payments on its securities at a fixed annual rate. However, dividends on common stock are at the discretion of the management of the firm (subject to restrictions embedded in debt covenants) and omission of dividends on preferred stock is not an occasion of default. More generally, corporations commonly make payments to claimholders which are not contractually obligated. To date, there has been relatively little examination of the determinants of discretionary payments by corporations, and little consideration of how such payments can be incorporated into a model of asset contingent valuation.

Two additional problems, well-known from studies of conventional contingent claims, are that the yield curve for sovereign debt is neither flat nor stationary and that the volatility of a firm's assets is not stationary and does not evolve as a deterministic process. Curing the first problem introduces additional risks related to changes in the level, slope, and curvature of the yield curve. Curing the second problem introduces a risk – random changes in volatility – for which there is no hedge and no readily observed market price.

It should be noted that these problems are also present in pricing call options on common stock. The problems are,

10. See footnote 2.

however, more significant in pricing longer-term corporate instruments.

## 3.2 Specifying the Boundary Conditions

Contingent claim models of corporate security values generally assume that a firm makes payments pursuant to its contractual obligations for as long as possible, and that the first breach of an obligation triggers liquidation or recapitalisation followed by distribution of cash and/or securities according to the priorities of its claims. This provides the basis for specifying 'boundary conditions' for the values of the claims.

This conceptualisation of default may be flawed for several reasons. First, covenants in bank loan agreements and private placements are sometimes, but not always, relaxed when involuntary breach appears imminent. Secondly, breach of a contractual obligation – including even non-payment of principal and/or interest – does not necessarily trigger filing of a bankruptcy petition (although it is likely to produce a privately negotiated recapitalisation if it does not lead to bankruptcy). Thirdly, reorganisation through bankruptcy is sometimes available to firms that are not experiencing difficulty meeting their current obligations. (I refer here to Johns Manville and A.H. Robbins.) Finally, even when recapitalisation follows default and bankruptcy, the distribution of securities in the recapitalised firm does not necessarily comport with the priorities of the original claim holders.[11]

---

11. Julian Franks and Walter Torous, 'An Empirical Investigation of US Firms in Reorganization', *Journal of Finance*, 44 (1989), pp. 747–69; Lawrence Weiss, 'Bankruptcy Resolution', *Journal of Financial Economics*, 27 (1990), pp. 285–314; Allan Eberhart, William Moore, and Rodney Roenfeldt, 'Security Pricing and Deviations from the Absolute Priority Rule in Bankruptcy Proceedings', *Journal of Finance*, 45 (1990), pp. 1457–69; and Allan Eberhart and Richard Sweeney, 'Does the Bond Market Predict Bankruptcy Settlements?', *Journal of Finance*, 47 (1992), pp. 943–80.

## 3.3 Other matters

A third problem with applying contingent claims analysis to
corporate securities is that maturing debt is often refinanced
by the sale of new debt or equity rather than paid off from the
assets of the firm. The implications of management discretion
in the choice of refinancing instruments has not yet been
incorporated in the valuation of securities which remain
outstanding through the refinancing process.

It should also be noted that discretionary dividend
payments to common shareholders and discretion in the
choice of refinancing instruments are only two aspects of the
larger topic of the consequences of management discretion for
debt and equity pricing. Although creditors and stockholders
hold contingent claims on a corporation, they do not rank
equally in their abilities to direct the affairs of the firm.
Stockholders, acting through management, can be expected
to engage in activities which enhance the value of their stock,
even when such activities reduce the market value of the
firm's debt. (Unless, of course, the activities are prohibited by
covenant.) This includes activities such as formation of
captive finance subsidiaries,[12] mergers and spin-offs,[13] and
negotiation of leveraged buyouts.[14] The discretionary ability
to engage prospectively in such activities can be expected to
enhance the *ex ante* value of the stock, and possibly reduce
the *ex ante* value of the debt, at any given value of the firm's
assets. Asset contingent valuation models do not now address
the management value associated with common stock.

12. E. Han Kim, John McConnell and Paul Greenwood, 'Capital
Structure Rearrangements and Me-First Rules in an Efficient Capital
Market', *Journal of Finance*, 32 (1977), pp. 789–810.

13. Dan Galai and Ronald Masulis, 'The Option Pricing Model and the
Risk Factor of Stock', *Journal of Financial Economics*, 3 (1976), pp. 53–81.

14. Paul Asquith and Thierry Wizman, 'Event Risk, Covenants, and
Bondholder Returns in Leveraged Buyouts', *Journal of Financial
Economics*, 27 (1990), pp. 195–213; and Leland Crabbe, 'Event Risk: An
Analysis of Losses to Bondholders and "Super Poison Put" Bond
Covenants', *Journal of Finance*, 46 (1991), pp. 689–706.

# 4. PROSPECTS

Asset contingent valuation does not presently offer a definitive methodology for valuing corporate securities. There are too many parameters (like dividends on common stock) whose values have to be inserted 'by hand', and some assumptions (like strict priority in bankruptcy and the absence of stockholder/management discretion) may be too crude for particular applications.

However, asset contingent valuation does provide an important focus for addressing the broad issues of securities pricing. It reminds us that loan covenants and bankruptcy law are crucial in controlling and resolving conflicts between different classes of claimholders, and it reminds us of the importance of underlying asset value. More particularly, it reminds us that debt and equity are not two easily distinguished classes of financial instruments, but rather are two pieces of a common puzzle.

Thus, we can probably expect to see more frequent applications of contingent claims analysis in pricing corporate securities. The applications will doubtless be crude at the outset, but will become more refined as practitioners become more familiar with the strengths and, more importantly, the shortcomings of the applications.

## Chapter 6

# CURRENT LEGAL AND REGULATORY DEVELOPMENTS AFFECTING THE DERIVATIVES MARKET

Alan Newton,
Freshfields

## 1. BACKGROUND TO CURRENT INTEREST

The derivatives markets have been the focus of considerable attention in the last 18 months or so. This has resulted from a number of factors, including firstly, increased awareness of the size and importance of these markets in the management of financial risks; secondly, their enormous profitability to the institutions which trade in them; thirdly, the relatively recent realisation on the part of the regulators of the need to understand fully the derivatives markets and to re-evaluate their approach to regulation.

Perhaps the catalyst for the upsurge in interest in the derivatives market was the much reported speech by Gerald Corrigan, president of the New York Federal Reserve Bank, in January 1992. His speech contained a strongly worded warning of the risks being run by banks and other participants in the derivatives markets, and their potential for adverse systemic consequences. His speech was seen as something of a rallying call to international regulators to look into these questions as a matter of some urgency.

The information and expressions of opinion in this chapter are not intended to be a comprehensive study, nor to provide legal advice, and should not be treated as a substitute for specific advice concerning individual situations.

## 1.1 Promisel Report

The Bank for International Settlements (BIS) commissioned a study, chaired by Mr Larry Promisel of the Board of Governors of the Federal Reserve, to look in particular at the growth of derivatives business and its implications for the interbank market. The Promisel Report was published in November 1992. It conducted a wide ranging review of the markets, drew attention to a number of issues, and made some broad suggestions concerning risk management practices, the improvement of the legal and institutional underpinnings of wholesale markets, the resolution of legal uncertainties, and the improvement of accounting and disclosure standards.

## 1.2 Bank of England Report

Following the Promisel Report, the Bank of England made its own internal study of derivatives activity in London and the risks being run by UK banks. The Securities and Futures Authority (SFA) also participated in this study. The Bank published its findings in April 1993 in the Report of the Bank of England Internal Working Group and its conclusions largely echoed those of Promisel.

## 1.3 Group of Thirty Study Group

The most recent report in this area was published in July of this year by the Group of Thirty, an informal Washington think-tank composed of market practitioners rather than regulators. The report sees its most important contribution as defining sound risk-management practices for derivatives dealers and end-users. The report highlighted one of the most notable characteristics of derivatives transactions which is that they frequently do not fit clearly within the current legal framework in the jurisdictions where transactions occur. Accordingly the report emphasised that dealers and end-users should continue to work together to evaluate developments in light of existing laws to assess what legal issues may arise. It also stressed that they should take the initiative to ensure that risks arising from these developments can be properly handled through analysis, market practices, documentation and, when necessary, legislation.

The report of the Group of Thirty identified the main legal risks which dealers perceive as affecting derivatives business and made a number of recommendations relevant to these risks. The report identifies five main legal risks that can occur at different stages of an over-the-counter derivatives trans-action. These are: (1) contract formation; (2) capacity; (3) insolvency and netting; (4) multibranch netting; and (5) legality.

The principal recommendations of the Group of Thirty report in relation to legal risk were:

RECOMMENDATION 21: RECOGNISING NETTING
Regulators and supervisors should recognise the benefits of netting arrangements where and to the full extent that they are enforceable, and encourage their use by reflecting these arrangements in capital adequacy standards. Specifically, they should promptly implement the recognition of the effectiveness of bilateral close-out netting in bank capital regulations.

The efficacy of netting arrangements is probably the principal legal issue currently occupying the market. This issue will be addressed in detail by other speakers.

RECOMMENDATION 22: LEGAL AND REGULATORY
UNCERTAINTIES
Legislators, regulators, and supervisors, including central banks, should work in concert with dealers and end-users to identify and remove any remaining legal and regulatory uncertainties with respect to:
    the form of documentation required to create legally enforceable agreements (statute of frauds);
    the capacity of parties, such as governmental entities, insurance companies, pension funds, and building societies, to enter into transactions (*ultra vires*);
    the enforceability of bilateral close-out netting arrangements in bankruptcy;
    the enforceability of multibranch netting arrangements in bankruptcy;
    the legality/enforceability of derivatives transactions.

These five main enforceability risks were analysed for nine major jurisdictions (Australia, Brazil, Canada, England, France, Germany, Japan, Singapore and the United States). The report recommended that regulators and legislators in these jurisdictions should remove the remaining uncertainties that have been identified and, in other countries, market participants, regulators, and legislators should work to identify and resolve any similar legal risks.

As previously mentioned, I will be looking at three specific aspects of the risks and uncertainties identified by the report – contract formation, capacity and legality.

### RECOMMENDATION 23: TAX TREATMENT

Legislators and tax authorities are encouraged to review and, where appropriate, amend tax laws and regulations that disadvantage the use of derivatives in risk management strategies. Tax impediments include the inconsistent or uncertain tax treatment of gains and losses on the derivatives, in comparison with the gains and losses that arise from the risks being managed.

The report noted that in many jurisdictions the tax treatment being applied to derivatives transactions dates back to before they came into general use. This can lead to considerable uncertainty in determining how gains and losses associated with these instruments should be taxed depending upon their use. This problem is true of the United Kingdom, where the tax treatment of derivatives has relied on discretionary treatment which has proved unsatisfactory for such a large and important market. I do not intend to look at the tax treatment of derivatives in the United Kingdom since it is a complex subject meriting detailed analysis. All I would say is that the United Kingdom process of legislative reform in the fiscal area has commenced. The Finance Act 1993 introduced changes to the taxation of foreign exchange gains and losses and in August 1993 the Inland Revenue produced draft legislation in respect of the taxation of both over the counter and exchange traded derivatives aimed at clarifying the tax position of such instruments.

One final introductory point – in choosing the law to govern a derivatives transaction, derivatives dealers are most likely to select the jurisdiction that provides the greatest legal certainty. It is comforting for UK practitioners to note that the Group of Thirty report indicated that the most commonly used law was English (53 per cent), the second most popular choice being New York (31 per cent). With regard to jurisdictions which caused dealers concern, some 53 per cent of dealers said that there were jurisdictions which caused them concern. However, only 2.5 per cent cited the United Kingdom as such a jurisdiction and only 5 per cent cited the United States. The jurisdiction which causes the greatest concern is apparently France.

For the United Kingdom this is a particularly noteworthy and reassuring response following so closely on the heels of the Hammersmith and Fulham swaps case. However, the Hammersmith and Fulham case clearly demonstrates that legal risks and regulatory concern as to legal uncertainty can still arise in jurisdictions which are generally well regarded.

## 2. CONTRACT FORMATION

The volume of derivatives transactions and the fact that they are concluded largely through telephonic or screen based dealing makes it important that the parties know that a binding contract is concluded when the deal is struck. This is particularly important because market prices change very quickly and because it may take some time to document the transaction. Documentation backlog has been a long-standing problem of the derivatives industry.

In the United Kingdom it is clearly established that a contract for derivatives does not need to be in writing. Accordingly, deals struck on the telephone are binding when they are struck (provided the requisite elements for formation of a contract are present) and there does not need to be a written agreement. The written confirmation sent after a transaction has been agreed in simply that – a confirmation of a contract which has been entered into.

This is not the case in all jurisdictions. For example concerns have been raised in the past in New York as to statute of frauds provisions in relation to certain types of derivatives contracts and efforts are being made to amend New York's statute of frauds.

Even in the United Kingdom the importance of reducing a contract to writing – in advance or in due course – should not be underestimated. Although the absence of writing does not prevent a contract from being formed, it certainly makes enforcement more difficult as there could be disagreements or uncertainties over the precise terms of the contract, although the tape recording of telephone conversations assists here. It may, for example, be necessary for a court to 'impute' certain terms into an oral contract – possibly on the basis of market practice – and these may be terms which one party would have preferred to modify in some way.

Sometimes an oral contract alone will not suffice. If a guarantee is to be provided, under the Statute of Frauds 1677 written documentation – either the guarantee or a written memorandum of it – will be necessary for the guarantee to be valid. Similarly written documentation is necessary for certain types of security interest to be effective.

# 3. CAPACITY

The decision of the House of Lords in *Hazell v Hammersmith and Fulham London Borough Council and Others* [1992] 2 A.C.1 focused attention both in the United Kingdom and internationally on capacity issues – not only for local authorities, but for a much wider range of counterparties.

'Capacity' is the basic legal ability to do a certain thing. Whilst an individual has unlimited capacity in the eyes of the law, the same is not generally true of persons created by the law. The problem is exacerbated by the fact that the capacity of many institutions to effect particular types of transaction was determined before modern derivatives emerged. The consequences of failing to ensure that a counterparty has the capacity to enter into a derivatives transaction was made crystal clear by the decision of the House of Lords in the Hammersmith and Fulham case which rendered void agreements between over 130 councils and over 75 of the world's largest banks. As activity in derivatives has increased, the range of counterparties effecting derivatives transactions has also increased. As a result of the Hammersmith and Fulham decision the participants in the derivatives market now look carefully at the capacity of governmental entities and other bodies regulated by legislation such as insurance companies and building societies, and also less frequently encountered counterparties such as pension funds and unit trusts where capacity is regulated by the terms of trust arrangements or by regulation.

Looking at certain entities in more detail:

## 3.1 Companies

A company's capacity is determined by the objects clause in its Memorandum of Association. In the case of a modern financial institution there may well be an express power to enter into derivatives transactions. Even in the absence of such a provision, a bank or financial institution is likely to have a widely drafted objects clause which should encompass derivatives transactions for risk management purposes. In the case of non-financial corporates, there is unlikely to be any express power. However, it may be possible to imply a power to enter into such transactions where they are entered for a proper purpose. Such a 'proper purpose' might be to hedge against risks to which the company is exposed in the ordinary course of its business, for example the risk of loss resulting from changes in interest or currency exchange rates. This power may be seen as incidental or conducive to the express powers of the company. By contrast, a company may not have implied power to enter into such transactions on a purely speculative basis with a view to profit.

## 3.2 Safe harbour

Following recent legislative changes, however, the capacity of registered companies to enter into derivatives transactions is no longer critical to a counterparty. The Companies Act 1989 introduced new safe harbour provisions into the Companies Act 1985 which substantially modified the *ultra vires* rule.

Section 35 provides that: '(1) The validity of an act done by a company shall not be called into question on the ground of lack of capacity by reason of anything in the company's memorandum'. Essentially this has the effect that the counterparty will not be prejudiced even if the entry into the transaction was outside the company's express or implied powers – the transaction will not be avoided.

Section 35A deals with the issue of whether the directors of the company may be taken by an outsider to have authority to bind the company, both in relation to a transaction which is within its capacity and where they purport to bind the company to enter into an *ultra vires* transaction. It provides that: '(1) In favour of a person dealing with a company in good faith, the power of the board of directors to bind the company, or authorise others to do so, shall be deemed to be free of any limitation under the company's constitution'.

Whilst this provision introduces the rather uncertain 'good faith' test in to the application of section 35, the test is not particularly stringent: a person is deemed to have acted in good faith unless the contrary is proved, and no person is to be regarded as acting in bad faith by reason only of his knowing that an act is beyond the powers of the directors under the Memorandum and Articles of Association.

Section 35A is limited in that it relates only to the power of the board of directors to bind the company or authorise others to do so. A third party dealing with an individual director or employee or arguably a committee of the board will not be protected by section 35A, and will have to rely on the common law principles of agency and ostensible authority. It is for this reason that a counterparty should require the production of a board resolution authorising the entry by the company into the proposed transaction (or authorising a named individual to determine whether such a transaction should be entered into).

The Companies Act 1989 also introduced section 35B into the Companies Act 1985. This supplements the above sections by providing that a party dealing with a company is not bound to enquire as to whether a proposed transaction is permitted by the company's constitution or as to any other limitation on the powers of the board to bind the company or to authorise others to do so.

## 3.3 Building societies

Building societies are statutory corporations regulated by the Building Societies Act 1986 (BSA). Section 23 of the BSA provides an express power to enter into hedging transactions – 'contracts of a prescribed description for the purpose of reducing the risk of loss arising from changes in interest rates, currency exchange rates or other factors of a prescribed description which affect its business'.

For this statutory power to be available to a society it must have been expressly adopted by a special resolution of the members of the society. In addition, in certain cases (although these have recently been reduced to less common types of derivatives transaction) the society must also satisfy a 'qualifying asset holding'. This requires the society to have total commercial assets, as shown in its annual accounts for the previous financial year, of not less than £100,000,000.

Once it is established that the society is qualified in general terms to enter into hedging transactions, each individual transaction should be considered, and in particular it must be determined:

(i) whether the transaction is a 'contract of a prescribed description'. The types of transactions which a society may enter into under the BSA are currently specified in the Building Societies (Prescribed Contracts) Order 1993 (the Order); and

(ii) whether the transaction is being entered for a proper purpose. Transactions which do fall within the provisions of the Order may only be entered for the purpose of reducing the risk of loss arising from changes in interest rates, currency exchange rates or other factors of a prescribed description which affect its business. If such transactions are entered into for another purpose, for example with a view to making a profit, they will be void. The issue in this context is therefore how the counterparty can know what the purpose of the society is in entering into the proposed transaction. The answer is of course that it cannot. The counterparty may be willing to proceed on the basis of the representations and indemnities which will usually be given by the society, however these may not be enforceable. Ultimately, there is no safe harbour for a counterparty acting in good faith.

## 3.4 Insurance companies

Most insurance companies are incorporated under the Companies Act 1985 and its predecessors. The factors which I have outlined in relation to companies generally will therefore be applicable, and third parties dealing with those companies will now benefit from the provisions introduced by the Companies Act 1989 and referred to above.

Some of the older insurance companies are however statutory corporations, incorporated under private Act of Parliament. Their capacity extends only as far as the express powers provided by the Act of Parliament which created them, and there is no protection for the counterparty if the transaction proves to be outside the capacity of the company or if the officer acting for the company has no authority to bind it. The provisions of the Act and any other constitutional documents should therefore be closely examined by the counterparty. In such a case the principles of statutory construction applied in the Hammersmith and Fulham judgment would be potentially relevant.

Whichever category the company falls within, the provisions of the Insurance Companies Act 1982, which authorises and regulates the carrying on of insurance business, will also need to be considered.

Section 16(1) of the Insurance Companies Act provides that an insurance company shall not carry on any activities otherwise than in connection with or for the purposes of carrying on its insurance business. It is unclear what the consequences would be if an insurance company was found to have acted for improper purposes, although it is thought unlikely that this would avoid any agreement entered into as a result. It is, however, advisable for a counterparty to seek confirmation that an insurance company is acting for the purposes of its insurance business. This expression has not been defined, but it is thought should include investing premium receipts and hedging resulting risks.

## 3.5 Local authorities

Local authorities are statutory bodies: they have only those powers which are specified in the legislation that creates and regulates them. Local authorities are regulated by the Local Government Act 1972, which provides that local authorities have the power to do anything 'which is calculated to facilitate, or is conducive or incidental to, the discharge of any of their functions'. The unanimous decision of the House of Lords in the Hammersmith and Fulham case was that local authorities do not have, and have never had, capacity to enter into rate protection transactions, *ie* swaps, caps, collars, floors, FRAs or similar transactions. It was held that, whilst local authorities have express statutory borrowing powers, there is no implied power to enter into derivatives trans-actions since such a power cannot be seen as incidental or conducive to those statutory powers. The House of Lords did not consider that debt management was one of the functions of a local authority. The House of Lords also held that all rate protection transactions entered into by a local authority involved an element of speculation, and that it was for Parliament to determine whether a local authority should have the capacity to enter into such transactions.

## 3.6 Unit trusts

Unit trusts are not separate legal entities and therefore cannot enter into any type of contract, including any derivatives transaction, on their own behalf. They must act through a trustee, who may in turn appoint an investment manager, to enter into such transactions on its behalf. The trustee will hold the benefit of all transactions on trust for the investors in the unit trust.

The power of the trustee to enter derivatives transactions (and to authorise others to do so on his behalf) will be set out in the trust deed and, in the case of authorised unit trusts regulated by the Securities and Investments Board (SIB) under the Financial Services Act 1986 (FSA). The regulations are now contained in the SIB's Regulated Schemes Regulations.

The law governing the capacity of unit trusts to enter into derivatives transactions is complex, and its application to particular transactions will depend on the structure of and parties to those transactions.

### 3.6.1 Where the trustee enters into the transaction

The counterparty will firstly need to be satisfied that the trustee itself has the capacity to act as a trustee and to enter into the relevant transaction. Where a trustee is a corporate trustee the counterparty will now benefit from the protection of the safe harbour provisions under the Companies Act 1985 (as amended).

Secondly, the counterparty must establish that the trustee has the power, under the terms of the relevant trust (contained in the trust deed and, in the case of an authorised unit trust, contained in the SIB Regulated Schemes Regulations), to enter into the relevant derivatives transactions for the account of the trust.

The trustee itself may be bound by the terms of the agreement if the first condition – as to the trustee's own capacity – is satisfied but, if the second condition – as to compliance with the terms of the trust and, where relevant, the SIB's Regulated Schemes Regulations – is not met, or indeed if the trustee is exercising its powers improperly, it will not be entitled to have recourse to the assets of the trust in meeting its obligations under that agreement. The credit risk taken on by the counterparty will then be fundamentally affected. It will inevitably be difficult for a counterparty to satisfy itself that a trustee is exercising its powers properly.

### 3.6.2 Where the trustee acts through an investment manager

The investment manager may act either as principal or agent. If it acts as principal, the capacity of the investment manager will be relevant: the counterparty need not be concerned with the capacity or power of the trustee. If the manager is a corporate, the counterparty will again benefit from the safe harbour provisions of the Companies Act 1985 (as amended).

If the manager acts as disclosed agent for the trustee, the capacity and powers of the trustee will again be relevant, as will the authority of the manager to bind the trustee. Common law principles of agency will apply.

For the investment manager itself, the capacity and powers of the trustee will always be relevant since they go to the question of the source of the investment manager's authority and the investment manager's rights of recourse against the trustee.

## 3.7 Pension funds

A pension fund is not a separate legal entity. Its assets will be vested in trustees and managed on their behalf by an investment manager. The general principles which I have outlined in relation to the capacity of the trustees of unit trusts to enter into derivatives transactions are equally applicable to pension funds.

There are of course many other types of entity the capacity of which needs to be carefully considered. This is particularly the case with overseas counterparties where local law advice should be obtained.

## 4. LEGALITY

## 4.1 Gaming

The application in certain jurisdictions of legislation intended to deal with gaming or wagering is the most common issue which gives rise to concerns about the legality of derivatives transactions because of the inherently speculative nature of many of such transactions and the failure of legislation to recognise the distinction between hedging and speculation. In the United Kingdom, the Gaming Acts have historically been a problem. However, following the enactment of section 63 of the Financial Services Act 1986, this is no longer a real concern. Section 63 provides that no contract entered into by either or each party by way of business and the making or performance of which by either party amounts to dealing in investments will be void or unenforceable as a result of the Gaming Acts.

Similar protection does not exist in many other jurisdictions and potential difficulties in relation to gaming or wagering should be borne in mind where another jurisdiction is involved.

## 4.2 Insider dealing

The insider dealing provisions of the Criminal Justice Act are designed to implement the Insider Dealing Directive, and will entirely replace the current legislation contained in the Company Securities (Insider Dealing) Act 1985. Many derivatives instruments which are outside the scope of the current legislation will be covered under the Criminal Justice Act. In broad terms, the derivatives instruments covered under the new legislation will include: futures and options contracts traded on LIFFE and OM (London) Limited; OTC options and futures on exchange-traded shares and debt instruments; OTC equity index options; and OTC equity-related swaps.

## 4.3 Money laundering

The money laundering provisions of the Criminal Justice Act 1993 and the Money Laundering Regulations will significantly increase the compliance requirements for banks and securities firms in this area and will be applicable to derivatives transactions. These provisions are designed to implement the Money Laundering Directive, which should have been implemented in the United Kingdom by 1 January 1993. Although the Act has now been passed, it will not come into force until, probably, the end of the year. The Regulations are due to come into effect on 1 April 1994.

## 4.4 Securities law compliance

It is of course crucial to ensure that the means adopted to do business are not contrary to any applicable securities or financial services legislation or regulations. In the United Kingdom this means in particular ensuring compliance with the FSA and any applicable self-regulatory organisation, or Bank of England, requirements.

## 4.5 Other

In some jurisdictions other legality issues, for example exchange control legislation or regulations may be relevant to certain types of transaction in derivatives.

# 5. SECURITY AND COLLATERAL

The taking of security for counterparty obligations and the complex issues which arise in connection with security interests was not an area particularly addressed by the Group of Thirty report, although it was discussed in some of the local enforceability surveys. The area is, however, one of increasing concern to market participants. Recent years have seen a marked 'flight to quality' so far as credit risk is concerned. Given the limited supply of good quality credits, participants have begun to look at other ways of addressing credit risk. The creation of AAA rated special purpose derivatives vehicles has been one route, but more simple to establish, and therefore more frequently encountered, are security or collateral arrangements. This development has also been accentuated by the tightening up of regulatory capital requirements.

For example, one of the current initiatives being driven forward by the International Swap Dealers Association (ISDA) is the development of a standard mark to market collateral agreement which counterparties could use in relation to transactions documented under the terms of the ISDA Master Agreement.

However, taking security raises a number of complex questions. These include:

(a) the nature of the asset being charged and the way in which it can be charged. For example, whilst in the United Kingdom almost any type of asset can be the subject of a security interest, difficulties have arisen under the case of *Re Charge Card Services Ltd.* [1989] Ch 497 in respect of a creditor taking security over its own obligations to a debtor – *eg* in relation to a bank deposit;

(b) the nature of the security interest and its effectiveness. For example, in English law the distinction between fixed and floating security interests is important. Also the remedies may vary depending on the nature of the security interest – the remedies of a legal mortgagee are different to those of an equitable chargee and the remedies of the holder of a floating charge are different to those of the holder of fixed security;

(c) registration and perfection requirements. In the United Kingdom certain types of security interest are registrable and registration is necessary to perfect the security as against a liquidator or administrator. Regulation is also notice to persons who may reasonably be expected to search the register;

(d) the consequences of failure to register or perfect security. In England failure to register a registrable security interest within the prescribed period will render it void against the liquidator, an administrator and any other creditor.

These issues apply to taking security from an English counterparty in England. However, the basic issues apply equally to taking security from an overseas counterparty or in an overseas jurisdiction, although obviously the local requirements and rules may be different.

In many jurisdictions certain types of insolvent reorganisation – *eg* administration in the United Kingdom and Chapter 11 in the United States – can result in a stay on enforcement of security, so even having valid security in place will not necessarily give an immediate remedy. In addition, in view of the impracticality of registering security interests in relation to derivatives assets, where the subject matter of the security interest may be constantly changing, and the difficulties some counterparties may have in relation to negative pledge obligations, structures using an outright transfer of title to assets (normally securities) used to support a counterparty's obligations, combined with an obligation to redeliver equivalent assets, may be a more flexible way forward. This approach has been adopted in the approved forms of stock lending agreements and in the Public Securities Association/ International Securities Association (PSA/ISMA) Global Master Repurchase Agreement. In arrangements of this kind in the event of counterparty default the parties rely on the monetary quantification of their respective rights and obligations in respect of the delivery or redelivery of securities or equivalent securities and rights of set-off to establish a net payment liability for one party. The effectiveness of set-off on insolvency of a counterparty will of course depend on the laws of the jurisdiction which governs the insolvency proceedings. In relation to these arrangements it is also necessary to address the issue of whether a court would be likely to recharacterise the transaction as a disguised secured loan. Following the recent decision of the Court of Appeal in *Welsh Development Agency v Export Finance Co Ltd.* [1992] BCC 270, in relation to English law this latter point is much less of a concern.

# 6. STANDARDISATION OF DOCUMENTATION

In relation to legal risk issues generally it is worth mentioning that one notable feature of OTC derivatives activity is the marked trend in favour of standardised even handed market documentation. This is particularly apparent in the field of swaps where, under the umbrella of ISDA, a sophisticated framework of documentation has been developed which has been extended from interest rate and currency swaps across a much wider range of derivatives products including caps, collars and floors, options and equity and commodity derivatives.

The development of standardised documentation has also been seen in relation to currency options, for example the International Currency Options Market (ICOM) terms, foreign exchange transactions – for example the FX Net standard terms and the British Bankers Association (BBA) International FX Master Agreement, and also the approved stock lending agreements and the PSA/ISMA Global Master Repurchase Agreement.

The importance of standard documentation was recognised in the Group of Thirty report both for the efficiencies it brings to the market, particularly in relation to documentation backlog, and the advantages it can create through effective netting provisions across different product ranges. The report recommended:

RECOMMENDATION 13: AGREEMENTS
Dealers and end-users are encouraged to use one master agreement as widely as possible with each counterparty to document existing and future derivatives transactions, including foreign exchange forwards and options. Master agreements should provide for payments netting and close-out netting, using a full two-way payments approach.

# 7. CONCLUSION

As with any kind of commercial or financial activity, derivatives transactions involve a degree of legal risk. However, perhaps because of the mathematical complexity of the hedging theories and risk management strategies associated with derivatives trading, there is an unwarranted degree of 'mythology' associated with derivatives. I do not consider that the legal risks associated with derivatives activity are any greater or any more complex than those associated with many other types of complex commercial or financial activity. I believe that this was recognised from a regulatory standpoint by the Bank of England in the Report of its Internal Working Group published in May 1993. The Bank said:

> ... there is little that can be clearly said to be unique about derivatives in so far as supervisory interest is concerned ... Derivatives mainly isolate and/or combine existing risks (albeit in shapes that may sometimes be more difficult to manage). Several of the problems exhibited by the markets are common to new activities ... This is not to say, of course, that a continuing and intensified focus on derivatives in unnecessary – the vast increase in derivatives activity and the need to constantly update our knowledge of market developments both indicate that this focus is justified. However, it needs to be borne in mind that a number of recommendations may equally well apply to trading activities as a whole rather than just derivatives.

*Chapter 7*

# COMPETITION FOR FUTURES AND DERIVATIVES MARKETS: THE ROLE OF REGULATION

Edward J. Swan,
Institute of Advanced Legal Studies

## 1. INTRODUCTION

By October of 1993 the total annual value of the products being traded on futures and derivatives markets was calculated to be at least tens of *trillions* of US dollars.[1] Futures and derivatives markets are tools of tremendous economic power. They have long been a source of competition between nations, and will continue to be so. The purpose of this chapter is to examine the nature of futures and derivatives, and to explore how they can be most effectively regulated to gain the advantages of that business for a regulating jurisdiction.

As a preliminary step, it is a good idea to consider what the means of competition is. That is to say, what is it that different regulatory jurisdictions offer in competition with one another in order to try to attract the business of futures and derivatives markets. In fact, what they are offering in competition with each other is freedom to contract.

Every derivative instrument is on a continuum ranging between a simple agreement to deliver a commodity in the future, where the parties intend that the commodity shall be delivered (usually called a 'forward contract') and an agreement to pay a party the future value of a commodity,

1. *OTC Derivative Markets and Their Regulation* (Washington: Commodity Futures Trading Commission, Oct. 1993), pp. 31–45.

85

a pure speculation. The extent of the range of contracts on that continuum that a regulator permits parties to enter into constitutes the extent of the freedom to contract permitted by that regulatory jurisdiction.

The product, this freedom to contract, consists, for purposes of derivative instruments, of two parts. First, the freedom to enter into these contracts which permits trade in future commodities; and, secondly, the freedom to transfer or assign these contracts to third parties. This second permits the creation of what are called 'contract markets' where trade is in the contracts themselves.

Permitting parties to enter into a wide range of futures and derivatives contracts confers a competitive trade advantage which increases revenue and control over commodities. Any state which offers freedom to contract derivative instruments gives itself an economic advantage which increases revenue from, and control over, the trading of commodities both for its merchants and for the state itself. This advantage works as follows. At its simplest level, it extends trade beyond commodities which are available now to commodities which are distant in time or geography.

## 1.1 Additional revenue

In terms of revenue this means that revenue is earned, in the present, not just on the sale of present commodities, but also on commodities to be delivered in the future. Of course, the expansion of revenue depends on the number of buyers willing to invest in future commodities, but experience has shown the revenue increase to be geometric. Futures markets usually trade 10–30 times the amount of the physical commodity ultimately produced in any delivery period, and in any futures market several delivery periods are usually being traded simultaneously. Theoretically, the further the delivery period of derivatives contracts extends into the future the more trade in futures commodities will be created, and the greater present market revenue will be. All of this trade creates not only direct revenue, presumably taxable, but also generates revenue for providers of ancillary support services.

In summary, the greater the extent of permissible derivative contracts over the previously discussed derivatives continuum, the larger the market will be, and the larger the potential revenue generated.

Indeed, derivative instruments which are underpinned by combinations of contracts and options build another layer of trade and revenue on already existing instruments. They enable the market to seek out not only customers for the general contracts offered on exchanges in great volumes, but individual clients with specific needs that cannot be met by large volume, general, futures and derivatives contracts.

## 1.2 Increased control of commodities

When considering how extensive the freedom to contract derivative instruments should be, it is not enough to consider the potential revenue that may be generated. The amount of control over the underlying commodities on which the contracts are written must also be considered. This control works as follows. At its most basic level, a market which offers to purchase future commodities will attract producers who want assurance of the future price of their production. These producers will choose to trade in markets which offer such futures contracts, giving those markets a commercial advantage over those markets that do not.

The attraction of future commodity production into a market gives the state regulating that market power over who can trade in the market, and under what circumstances. This translates into the opportunity to exercise control over the pricing and distribution of the commodities in question. This extension of control is not limited simply to ordinary futures contracts, but is a product of any derivative instrument that triggers the making of contracts for future delivery of any commodity. The broader the range of instruments a jurisdiction allows to be traded, the greater the range of business over which that regulating jurisdiction will exercise control.

Gaining that control depends on the nature of the regulation exerted over futures and derivatives trading.

## 2. REGULATION OF FUTURES AND DERIVATIVES

With futures and derivatives trading, as with any other economic activity, the government can choose whether to regulate it or not regulate it. 'Regulation' as it is used in this chapter is not intended to refer to general regulatory or tax provisions that also have affects on futures and derivatives trading. It will refer only to instances where the government has focused specifically on futures and derivatives contracts, by defining them for purposes of regulation, and acted with respect to that government-defined activity.

'Regulation' itself is often described as having 'interference' as its central element, in the sense that the government is interfering with what would otherwise be purely private transactions. Such interference can intend either to inhibit or encourage futures and derivatives trading. It can effect the formation of the contract or the contract result.

If it is the wish of the government to inhibit futures and derivatives contracts, regulation is relatively simple. Depending on how strongly the government opposes futures and derivatives contracts, it may affirmatively act to prevent them by making participating in such contracts a crime, subject to one or more penalties, or it may passively refuse to assist parties in futures and derivatives trading by declaring such contracts unenforceable at law.

If the government has determined to encourage futures and derivatives trading then the range of possible actions is much greater.

### 2.1 Definitions: spot transactions and time bargains

The first step in regulation is definition. Depending on the definition, a certain kind of contract is differentiated from other commercial contracts and deemed subject to special treatment.

Definition of the term 'futures contract' is not an easy task. Courts, regulators and private parties have had a difficult time getting their minds around the idea for centuries, so it is worth taking some time to understand what is being talked about. In general terms, without yet getting into the specific differences that are found in the legal definitions of different nations, there are certain characteristics that have generally been held to apply to all futures contracts. First, they are all for the sale of 'commodities', a term which is defined as 'everything of value that is produced. Commodities may be either goods or services',[2] or, more generally:

A kind of thing produced for use or sale, an article of commerce, an object of trade; in pl. goods, merchandise, wares, produce. Now esp. food or raw materials, as objects of trade; staple commodity: leading articles of trade'.[3]

This restriction to commodities excludes certain kinds of property which can also be objects of sales such as: real property, persons, livestock, public or private office, and various kinds of rights or duties. Essentially, the commodities referred to in any discussion of commodity futures trading are categories of moveables in commerce. The definition excludes those unique objects produced to be desired solely for themselves such as paintings by master artists, custom-built houses, or tailor-made suits. Nor does it include commodities sold to an ultimate consumer for personal use in his private or business life. The categories of commodities which are the subjects of commodity futures contracts are commodities of which there is a market for a future supply, usually for commercial purposes. This distinguishes futures contracts from a variety of other executory contracts[4] where the object of sale is also to be delivered in the future. Commodity futures contracts do not deal with transactions of one-off sales of particular commodities to meet individual needs a

2. Richard G. Lipsey, *An Introduction to Positive Economics*, 7th ed. (London: Weidenfeld & Nicholson, 1989), p.780.

3. OED, s.v., 'commodity'.

4. In classical contract law, wholly unperformed and unrelied upon contracts, which consist of mutual promises to perform in the future. P.S. Atiyah, *An Introduction to the Law of Contract,* 4th ed. (Oxford: Clarendon Press, 1989), p. 22.

particular times. As a contract form, it is a business tool of the market of future commodity supply.

## 2.1.1 Contracts for relations and transactions

Looked at in the terms of a number of modern contract law theorists, futures contracts fall into the category of contracts that are 'relations' rather than 'transactions'.

> A typical transaction is a discrete event, for instance a one-off sale between a buyer and seller who are never likely to meet again – say a motorist buying petrol at a filling station remote from his home. It is a once for all transaction, over and done with on the spot, as soon as the petrol-tank has been filled and the price paid. On the other hand, many contracts are not like this at all; they are long-term relationships, such as contracts of employment, or business relationships between long-standing suppliers and customers.[5]

This ties in with another important characteristic of commodity futures contracts, which is that they are contracts for the delivery of commodities in the future. However, the definition of what constitutes delivery 'in the future' varies from market to market and is not dependent purely on considerations of time. For an agreement to deliver a commodity in the future to be a 'futures contract', the agreement must provide for delivery, not only at a time later than the time the agreement is entered into, but at a time later than the period within which delivery is considered, in the relevant market, to constitute a 'spot' transaction.

## 2.1.2 Spot transactions

The term 'spot' transaction originated as a description of transactions that were completed 'on the spot' by immediate exchange of the purchase price and the object of sale. However, as market transactions became more complex, the term came to be applied to transactions where delivery of the

5. Atiyah, 55–6. Also see, Ian Macneil, 'Relational Contract: What We Do and Do Not Know', *Wisconsin Law Review* (1985), pp. 483, 505.

purchased commodity was expected within the shortest practicable time after the transaction had been concluded. This could be the amount of time it takes to move the commodity to the agreed place of delivery, or even the time it takes to produce the commodity. In more formal commodity markets the periods within which spot transactions can be completed by delivery was often limited to specific periods such as: two days (modern foreign exchange market),[6] 30 days (many commodity markets), or 'the current delivery period'. For example, the Chicago Board of Trade offers futures contracts for delivery of wheat in July, September, December, March and May. During the month of May, in that market, May would be the 'spot' month. In the absence of a prescribed period, the period within which a spot transaction must be completed is usually held to be 30 days.

Consequently, it is not time alone that distinguishes 'spot' transactions from futures contracts, but the intentions of the parties. In essence, a spot transaction is simply an agreement to sell and deliver commodities in the shortest practicable time (or within the time recognised in the market as the shortest practicable time). Time is more an accident of the physical circumstances of providing the commodity, than a desired element of the parties' relationship. In the context of contract law analysis, an agreement for spot delivery falls into the category of being a 'transaction' in the sense that the intentions of the parties are to exchange commodities for payment, with time serving only as the measure of the period required to complete the transaction.

### 2.1.3 Time bargains

At a more sophisticated level are found agreements in which a longer time period for performance than is necessary for a spot transaction is a desirable, even essential, condition. In seventeenth and eighteenth century England, such contracts were appropriately called 'time bargains'. This category

---

6. *Central Bank Survey of Foreign Exchange Market Activity* (Basle: Bank for International Settlements, 1993), p. 16.

encompasses modern 'forward', 'futures', and 'derivatives' contracts. What distinguishes the time bargain agreement from a spot transaction is that a longer time to complete the contract is not merely an accident of circumstance, but it is an essential condition of the contract, an important consideration for the parties to enter the agreement. The effect of adding a longer completion time to the other considerations in the agreement is that the agreement becomes no longer simply a 'transaction' to make payment for and deliver commodities, but the keystone of a contract of 'relationship' between the parties. This is because the agreement to keep the contract uncompleted for a length of time encompasses a range of possible alternative relations between the parties at the expiration of the contract term. The buyer of the commodity may, during the time allotted, raise the capital needed to complete the purchase, or he may find an alternative buyer acceptable to the seller to whom he can transfer his right to take delivery of the commodity, or he may find a buyer who wishes to purchase from him after he takes delivery. The seller, on the other hand, is given an opportunity to find a supply of a commodity he does not yet possess, or to sell what he does possess and purchase a cheaper acceptable commodity to deliver to the buyer, or to find a seller acceptable to the buyer, who will (at the time appointed in the agreement) deliver the specified commodity to the buyer.

What is being bargained for is not only a commodity, but the opportunity for the parties to change their relationship to the commodity and to each other before the time of performance. The promises exchanged, while based on the sale and purchase of a commodity, are promises by each party to guarantee the performance of one side of the transaction or the other, for a fixed period of time, giving the other party time to choose among the available alternatives for future completion of the contract. That promise, which is in essence a promise to keep a relationship of obligation open over a future period, while the parties consider the relative values of alternative methods of performance, not necessarily related to the availability of the underlying commodity, takes these 'time bargain' contracts out of the category of being merely 'transaction' contracts (such as 'spot' contracts are) and places them in the category of being 'relationship' contracts.

Although all time bargain contracts are today usually included within the term 'futures' contracts, there are at least three different kinds of time bargains, of which futures contracts is one.

### 2.1.3.1 Forward contracts

The first and least complicated kind of time bargain is the 'forward' contract. For reasons concerning the interests of the parties in particular cases, there has been a great deal of modern confusion (particularly in court cases in the United States)[7] about what the term means and whether it can be distinguished from futures contracts. In essence, a forward agreement is a time bargain in which the parties intend to limit their contractual relationship to making and taking delivery of the underlying commodity at a date in the future. In the event that it becomes necessary for one party or the other to find an alternative means of settling the contract before the time for performance (such as the buyer offering another buyer in his place), that is the result of particular circumstances. It usually requires the express permission of the other party to a variation in the agreement. Most importantly, it is not a result of the parties intention that the agreement was to be (in addition to a contract to supply a commodity in the future) a vehicle for speculation on which of a contemplated variety of alternative methods of settlement would be the most valuable at the date for performance.

Of course, there are inherent difficulties in proving the intentions of the parties in the event of a dispute. The written contractual documents are often an inaccurate or incomplete reflection of the parties intentions, or even of the usual course of dealing in commodities for which there is a continuous market. Consequently, legal systems which make policy distinctions between 'forward' contracts and other varieties

---

7. See, eg *Transnor (Bermuda) Limited v BP North America Petroleum, et al.*, 738 F. Supp. 1472 (SDNY 1990), and the cases citing it.

of time bargains[8] add to the legal costs of time bargain trading by imposing on courts the time-consuming burden of sifting the evidence to determine whether it supports a conclusion that original intentions of the contracting parties were to transfer commodities, rather than to speculate in changes in the commodity's value prior to delivery time.

## 2.1.3.2 Futures contracts

The most familiar type of time bargain agreement is called the 'futures contract'. This type of agreement differs from the 'forward' contract because the parties intend, at the time the contract is made, to have the right to settle the contract either by making or accepting delivery or by other settlement methods such as (depending on the regulations or practices of the particular commodity market) selling their rights and duties under the contract to another party, or paying the difference in the value of the contractual commodity between the time it was concluded and the time for performance. Contracts which specify, or permit, the latter settlement method are a subcategory of futures contracts called 'contracts for differences'.

Unlike the forward contract, the futures contract intentionally provides the parties with an opportunity to speculate in changes in the price of the underlying contractual commodity. In some jurisdictions the permitted speculation has historically been limited only to the right to transfer a party's rights under the contract, with contracts for differences held to be illegal or unenforceable because they constitute gambling contracts rather than real agreements to buy or sell commodities.

## 2.1.3.3 Derivative instruments

The newest category of time bargain agreements is called 'derivative instruments'. A derivative instrument is any contract, the value of which fluctuates according to the value of an underlying commodity or group of commodities. This definition is very broad and encompasses futures and

8. Such as the US Commodity Exchange Act.

forward contracts which have already been discussed. The term is used to describe stock-index based futures ('equity derivatives') and financial contracts offered for sale on established commodity exchanges, as well as privately offered, custom-designed contracts, not traded on exchanges, which offer price protection (in exchange for a fee) against fluctuations in the value of several commodities. For example, a financial services company might offer to an airline a contract guaranteeing that the airline will be provided with jet fuel, within a specified price range, over the next ten years.

There is no clear distinction between futures contracts and derivative instruments. However, the term 'futures contract' is usually applied to standardised commodity contracts traded on exchanges, whereas the term 'derivative instrument' is more likely to denote a custom-designed contract, not offered in standardised form on an exchange. Derivative instruments have become increasingly important. In the early 1990s the offering of derivative instruments by banks and other financial services companies grew from an obscure speciality to a multi-trillion dollar worldwide business. This has caused considerable concern among regulators because most of this business is conducted privately, off-exchange, out of the sight and supervision of government regulators. This raises concerns about the true size of the business, and whether the financial institutions dealing in derivative instruments are taking on greater levels of risk than they can sensibly carry.

## 3. THE USES OF FUTURES AND DERIVATIVES CONTRACTS

In the course of deciding whether it is desirable for a regulatory jurisdiction to make an effort to attract futures and derivatives markets, it is useful to examine the purposes for which such contracts can be used.

It is often said that futures and derivatives contracts are used either to 'hedge' or to 'speculate'. A time bargain is entered into for purposes of 'hedging' if its principal purpose is protection against future price changes. It is considered to be for 'speculating' if the parties hope to profit from future commodity price changes. However, useful as this analysis is, it obscures the principal purpose of time bargain contracts, which is to control commodities.

Historically, the device of the time bargain contract came into being for the purpose of promoting two relationships which gave control over commodities:

(1) financing future commodity production; and
(2) securing future commodity supply.

Once these two contractual relationships had been successfully established, time bargain contracts promoted a third device which extended control over commodities: the establishment and regulation of commodity markets.

Although the terms 'hedging' and 'speculating' could possibly be stretched to include functions of supporting future commodity production, or securing future commodity supply, those functions of time bargains are only by-products of the principal function of exerting control over commodities.

## 3.1 Control by financing future commodity production

Futures contracts operate as extensions of credit to producers of commodities. In their most ancient form, they consisted of payments of seed corn made in exchange for the promised delivery of future grain crops. It was a short step from that to payments of gold or silver in exchange for promises of future crops and finally, to promises to buy future crops at an agreed price. Each contract provided the producer with something of present value in exchange for his promise to deliver future commodity production.

At its most basic level of control, the very existence of the futures contract can provide a producer with the means to produce commodities that he might not otherwise be able to produce. At a more sophisticated level, futures contracts can be used to influence which commodities will be produced and sold. Those commodities for which producers have access to the credit facility of the futures contract will have an advantage over those commodities for which futures contracts are not available. Consequently, the availability of futures contracts exerts a level of control over such elements of natural resource commodity production as:

(1) what commodities will be produced,
(2) whether locally produced or foreign commodities will be sold in domestic markets, and
(3) whether some commodities will be cheaper than others because the risks of producing them are reduced.

## 3.2 Securing supply and control of natural resources

The opportunity to use futures contracts also gives advantages to buyers in securing future supplies of commodities. Those buyers who can employ futures contracts in their dealings with commodity suppliers can get the suppliers to commit future commodity supplies at known prices. Such contracts protect buyers against disruptions of supply or future price rises.

In addition, the availability of such contracts exerts control over commodities to be produced in the future by predetermining the direction of their flow to those buyers that use futures contracts. Futures contractors can buy ahead of their competitors. Futures contracts allow them to get to the supply of futures contracts first, at a price they can afford.

Futures trading also expands control over the volume of commodities in that futures trading includes sales not only of commodities now available in the spot market, but also of commodities distant in time or geography. Consequently, futures markets influence a much greater volume of commodities than markets that trade only spot commodities.

## 3.3 The establishment of commodity markets and control of commodities

The purchase and sale of commodities generates revenue. To the extent that commodities are sold pursuant to futures contracts, jurisdictions that encourage futures markets will enjoy that revenue. Consequently, the choices that any regulatory jurisdiction makes to encourage the creation and expansion of futures markets, will give that jurisdiction a degree of control over the revenue of commodity trading that jurisdictions declining to make those choices will not have.

If futures contracts are available in a particular jurisdiction as a means of financing future commodity production, those producers that want take advantage of that method of financing will come to that jurisdiction to do business. The result is a market in future commodities and, if the law allows assignment of contracts, in commodity futures contracts.

The existence of a futures market generates numerous financial benefits. At the first level there is the revenue realised directly from the purchase and sale of future commodities. Secondly, there is revenue and employment generated from the services and facilities used by the market traders. All of those financial benefits, and the revenue they create, come within the control of the jurisdictions doing the most to encourage futures trading.

In terms of control, jurisdiction over a futures market gives a regulatory authority the power to determine who will be permitted to participate in that market, and under what circumstances. In other words, the regulator controls the number and type of buyers in the market, the times and circumstance of sale, the degree of contract enforcement, and, consequently, influences the price of the commodities sold.

## 4. THE SHAPE OF FUTURES REGULATION

Any governmental jurisdiction is usually faced with a myriad of choices to make about which activities it wishes to encourage, and which it considers it wise to discourage. If, to gain the advantages discussed above, a regulatory regime decides to encourage futures trading then it has choices to make about what the shape of regulation should be, and what kind of regulation will most encourage beneficial market development.

# 4.1 Regulating to influence market location

Futures trading has a long history. Surveying the list of important futures markets over that history shows that the location of the markets is not determined by the location of commodity production, the location of consumption, or by the location most convenient port for shipping or distributing the commodity. For example, England produces no cocoa and is only the (distant) fifth largest consumer, yet London has the world's largest market for cocoa and cocoa futures.

In general, the principal determinant of market location of any particular product is transaction cost. 'Cost' involves a number of direct and indirect elements that contribute to the attractiveness, or lack of it, of any particular location. Among the direct costs are:

(1)  license fees;
(2)  taxes;
(3)  usage fees;
(4)  market rent;
(5)  accommodation costs;
(6)  commercial space rents;
(7)  middleman costs; and
(8)  regulation charges.

These direct charges are easily measurable costs of doing business which it is possible to add up and compare with other locations where it is possible to do the same business. However, there are also a number of indirect costs, which although they may not be as directly measurable as the costs listed above, nevertheless contribute to the transactions costs which make a particular market location more or less desirable. These include:

(1)  language differences;
(2)  convenience of time zone;
(3)  safety of persons and property;
(4)  market experience;
(5)  worker availability;
(6)  currency controls;
(7)  import/export barriers;

(8) legal costs;
(9) regulatory burden, and
(10) the overall ease of market entry, and of continued market participation.

To some extent, each of these costs varies according to location. The overall function of government regulation is to increase or decrease the total transaction costs of trading futures and thus to make it more or less desirable to trade futures contracts in the regulated jurisdiction.

There are several regulatory systems that governments can impose, each of which adds its own burdens and costs to the business of futures trading. Historically, those that have been tried, or that are in effect now, do not always have as much to do with encouraging or discouraging the business as they do with solving other political problems. However, in respect of any market that functions under a government, some form of government determination affects the transaction cost. Generally, the types of regulation chosen by government fall into two categories: passive regulation, and active regulation.

## 4.2 Types of government regulation

The existence of government imposes government regulation. It might be said that in respect of time bargain regulation government always has the choice not to regulate that type of business. However, this is a more complex concept than it appears on the surface. Assuming that any government needs some revenue to function and that economic activity of some kind must be enlisted to generate that revenue, it can be argued that choosing to raise revenue from certain activities, and not others, is a decision by government to make those government-revenue-raising activities bear the costs of providing government services to those non-government-revenue-raising activities that fall within a government's political jurisdiction. In other words, a decision 'not to regulate' can be seen as, in effect, a decision to grant a public subsidy to the 'unregulated' activity. Consequently, for purposes of this chapter it may not be valid to divide government action towards futures markets between 'regulated' and 'unregulated'. It is probably more accurate to classify types of government involvement as 'passive' or 'active' regulation. As shown below, there may also be other reasons why it is not possible to accurately describe any futures trading as 'unregulated'.

## 4.2.1 Passive government regulation

In respect of time bargains, 'passive regulation' covers circumstances in which the government has not imposed regular and specific supervision of time bargain business. However, this lack of regular supervision still leaves time bargains governed by various types of regulation including judicial and unmandated self-regulation.

### 4.2.1.1 Judicial regulation

The imposition of judicial regulation on time bargain business is determined by contract law. Time bargains are types of contracts. Judicial regulation comes into existence in those instances where questions of the enforceability of such contracts come before the courts. Basically, this involves issues of whether and how time bargain contracts are enforceable, or assignable. The circumstances under which they are determined by contract law, and determination of how agreements conform to the contract law standards of society is usually left to the courts.

The necessity of having to use the courts to make these decisions, and the types of decisions the courts make, add to the cost of using such contracts. Consequently, one regulatory decision open to government is whether a less expensive form of dispute resolution should be mandated for time bargain contract disputes.

### 4.2.1.2 Unmandated self-regulation

For several reasons, including protection against fraud, a desire to restrict competition, and continuity of practice, the traders in certain markets often feel that it is in their interests to collectively define and enforce a common standard of business practices and market participation requirements. This desire to introduce self-regulation may not be mandated by government, but it is still subject to a number of government regulations not specifically aimed at the market. For example, the standard of conduct required by self-regulation may be affected by general contract law, or anti-monopoly statutes.

Such market-driven self-regulation is affected by passive government regulation to the extent that government permits the self-regulation to function. For example, members of the London Stock Exchange of the nineteenth century were subject to a code of practice that ran afoul of more than one general contract law statute (such as Sir John Barnard's Law forbidding time bargains in shares), but the government allowed the Stock Exchange to rule itself, largely without interference, because it was thought to maintain beneficial standards of business conduct.

The principal advantage of market-driven self-regulation is the detailed knowledge that traders have about the ways their markets function, both publicly and in private. This knowledge is a tool that can be used to realistically regulate market behaviour that may be denied to government regulators for reasons of restrictive procedural requirements or lack of market experience.

### 4.2.1.3 Active government regulation

Active government regulation falls into several categories that can be described in different ways. The most comprehensive attempt thus far to define and describe the methods of regulation, and to summarise previous studies of the subject is found in Barry M. Mitnick, *The Political Economy of Regulation: Creating, Designing, and Removing Regulatory Forms* (New York: Columbia University Press, 1980).

Active regulation by government, in respect of time bargains, consists of identification of a particular market or market segment, and the taking of specific steps to control its activities. The steps of active government regulation are implemented by some legislative act of the government. The legislation can either impose new duties, specific to a particular market on existing government agents, or designate new government agents to handle the new regulation. The areas of time bargain activity affected by active government regulation can be identified as falling into three categories: (1) market entry, (2) market conduct, and (3) market result. At each stage the regulation can have either a direct financial effect (in the form of a tax, license fee, direct subsidy, tax concession or bonus etc), or a control on the scope of market activity (regardless of whether it seeks to limit or expand market participation). The regulatory function, when it is delegated to specific officials with the express task of regulating specific market activity, can be structured in a number of ways. It can be performed by a legislative committee. This was said to be a common method of regulation early in US history.[9] It can be turned over to private interests in the form of a franchise, concession or monopoly to exercise varying degrees of control over a particular market activity. The regulating can be performed by a commission, made up of a number of experts aided by an administrative staff, or a 'bureau' structured with a pyramidal administrative staff.

*Phases of regulatory agency evolution*
Several articles and books dealing with regulation have argued that there are discernible evolutionary stages in the life of any regulatory agency. Generally, there is an attempt to fit the life of a regulatory agency into at least four distinct stages of progress which are: (1) creation of the agency, (2) the growth of the agency, (3) the mature functioning of the agency, (4) the decline of the agency's function. These stages have been described as having historically progressed through stages described as 'promotional', 'competitive', 'monopolistic', and 'national co-ordination'. However, in addition to these stages commentators have also identified a stage of development which raises a different issue: that of 'capture'.[10]

9. Mitnick, p. 24.
10. See Mitnick, generally.

*The issue of capture*

'Capture' is defined as that period when regulators cease to serve the public interest and begin to serve the interests of the regulated.[11]

The existence of 'capture', and whether it is an inevitable, or even identifiable, stage of public regulatory agency life is a complex question. The issue of capture assumes that there is conflict between the interests represented by the regulatory agency, and those regulated. This conflict is usually identified as existing between the 'public interest' which the agency is created to protect, and the narrower private interests of the regulated. Of course, those political economists who discuss capture concede that a regulatory agency is created to promote, foster and expand the business of the regulated, and capture is not an issue. Capture becomes an issue when the agency is created to perform public duties which conflict with the private interests of the regulated. There is a question of whether the use of the term 'capture' tells us anything more than the word 'corruption' about the relationship between public officials and their duties. Corruption is generally defined as the perversion or destruction of integrity in the discharge of public duties by bribery or favour. Certainly, corruption is one way capture can occur, but it may not be the only way. Corruption would cover those situations where a regulatory agency puts the interest of the regulated ahead of the public interests in exchange for some specific bribe. Capture covers the broader situation where for ideological reasons, or for reasons of general professional advancement, regulators decide to favour the interests of the regulated to the detriment of the public duties which they were originally assigned.

What the commentators have generally concluded is that government regulators undertake their duties for a variety of reasons, and that agencies they work for have lives which usually pass through several different stages of effectiveness in carrying out the duties they were assigned.

11. Mitnick, pp. 89–94.

## The impact of government regulation

It is important for governments to realise, when deciding to form agencies for the regulation of market activities, including time bargain trading, that such agencies have a life of their own, quite independent of the industry they are regulating. The agency life cycle sometimes contributes to fulfilling the agency's regulatory mandate, and sometimes does not. What is certain is that it contributes to the costs of the business regulated. How these costs are distributed has important implications for expanding or discouraging the business in question.

If the regulatory agency is funded from general government revenues then it can be argued that this cost of the time bargain business is receiving a subsidy from the general population. Whether this subsidy is cost-effective depends on how effectively the agency is accomplishing its task of protecting the public interests in the regulated market. As the studies have shown, even in cases where the regulator is set up to be a purely independent public agency, there are likely to be time when the agency is 'captured' into promoting private interests at the expense of public interests. Consequently, it is difficult to argue that the creation of 'independent' public agencies is necessarily the most effective method for regulating futures market trading.

The difficulty faced by a government determined to employ active regulation is finding a way to strike a balance between achieving the objects of regulation without wasting effort on inefficient regulators.

## Achieving the objects of active regulation

A preliminary question which a government should carefully consider before choosing the type of regulation is: what are objects of active regulation? If the overall object is to encourage the growth of time bargain trading, then the objects of time bargain regulation can be identified as four:

(1)  raising revenue;
(2)  protecting market integrity;
(3)  preventing fraud; and
(4)  maintaining market confidence.

## 4.2.1.4 Self-regulation

Performing any of these tasks efficiently is aided by a detailed knowledge of the regulated markets. To a certain extent, such knowledge can be gained over time by outside regulators without practical market experience, but a more direct source of such knowledge is the market participants themselves. They also have the advantage of being in touch with changes in the market as they occur. This raises the question of whether some form of self-regulation is best.

In addition to market knowledge, self-regulation also offers some advantages of cost. To the extent that market participants are required to devote their own resources, time and money to overseeing the smooth functioning of the markets, the costs of regulation are paid directly by them. This takes the burden of paying for supervision off of the public generally, and solves the problem of an invisible subsidy being paid to run the markets.

On the other hand, if the costs of regulation are charged to the regulated (in the form of special taxes, license or usage fees) there is a direct increase to market transaction costs, which may make other market locations more appealing. Consequently, charging the costs of regulation directly to the market may make the market location less appealing than competing locations, unless it is compensated by the reduction of other transaction costs such as taxes, or labour, transportation and material costs. Increased trans-action costs are likely to cost the regulating jurisdiction business volume, and with that decline, loss of jobs and revenue.

Therefore, in respect of the goal of raising revenue, careful attention must be paid to the effect of any regulation costs on the total costs of market transactions.

The big complaint about self-regulation is that the regulators are already 'captured'. That is, they are chosen from the regulated and cannot help but have interests in promoting the objectives of the regulated. This situation may certainly help to increase revenue by attracting additional business to the markets, but it causes difficulties both in achieving market integrity and in maintaining market confidence.

In order to use self-regulation to achieve market integrity, the self-interests of the market trading regulators must be balanced by other interests. Among the interests are the fact that self-regulators will wish to prevent traders from leaving the market so they do have a self-interest in preserving market integrity. To the extent that those chosen to regulate are subject to the control of market participants as a whole, there is a counterbalance to narrow self-interest. The interests of the market members as a whole will be to preserve market integrity in order to protect the continuation of their business. In that case, the market as a whole may be able to construct sufficient sanctions against the failure of self-regulators to perform their regulatory duties. However, the power of the entire market over the regulators is limited by the individual market power of the regulators. Self-regulation, supervised by the market as a whole may not always be sufficient to preserve market integrity.

Nor may it always be adequate even to encourage market expansion. Those already in the market may have interests in keeping new traders out, and in limiting market growth, in order to protect their own positions.

In summary there are perhaps too many pitfalls to rely solely on self-regulation to promote the objects of active government regulation. Some form of government intervention must also be employed, at least in conjunction with self-regulation. There are various levels of government intervention possible. Statutory regulation, left to judicial enforcement, is the least subject to 'capture' and the threat of judicially imposed statutory punishment does act as a sanction against fraud and violations of market integrity (such as illegal combinations, corners, squeezes and price manipulation). This level of intervention has the advantage that the judiciary is likely to be more independent of the market trading community than dedicated government regulatory agencies or self-regulation panels. It suffers the disadvantage that the judiciary may need education about how the trading is done. Still, this is no more a disadvantage than it is in respect of any other business where the courts are asked to judge the rights and duties of participants. The real problems relating to the effectiveness of this form of supervision relate to statutory definition of rights and duties, and to court access.

In order for courts to understand what issues they are required by statute to consider, some careful drafting is required in order to assure that the concerns the government has about the conduct of the markets in question get a hearing before the court and that issues that the government does not wish them to consider remain off the judicial calendar. The government should determine how much discretion should be left to the court, and how much detail the statute should give to define the regulated activity. Because of the constantly changing nature of the futures markets, a balance should be struck between not restricting the courts' ability to deal with new modes of doing business, and giving them too little guidance about the nature of their mandate.

## 4.3 Certain regulatory functions can be exported

The regulation of futures trading attracts business to particular markets to the extent that the traders are provided with security, justice and profit. In some jurisdictions the provision of these three essential services is, for one reason or another, difficult or impossible and this causes the business to move elsewhere with a consequent decline in state revenue. This raises the question of whether the business can be encouraged by exporting some regulatory services to countries where it is easier to perform them, without losing the business of the futures markets.

### 4.3.1 Dispute resolution

In particular, a service that may be exportable is dispute resolution. In respect of some emerging countries, particularly former republics of the USSR, it is said that one of the problems in doing business there is official corruption. This would make potential traders leery of doing business there, because of the uncertainty of obtaining an impartial hearing in the event of a dispute. This fear of the effects of corruption could seriously hamper market development in those countries where it is believed to be a problem. In those countries where such corruption exists the market effect is that it adds to the costs doing business,[12] and may negate any other cost advantages offered to traders in developing countries.

One way around this problem is to remove dispute resolution from the reach of market location corruption. This can be done by having disputes resolved in another country, or by judicial panels from other countries. In effect, dispute resolution could be exported, and thus increase rather than diminish market trading. In the present international environment of futures trading this could be done in several ways. Many futures trading companies operate in markets all over the world, and most do business in the United Kingdom and the United States, the two most important futures trading nations. Consequently, such companies could include choice of law and submission to jurisdiction clauses in their contracts which would, in many cases, give them the right to have any resulting contract disputes determined in the chosen jurisdiction. Another method of dispute resolution export is by arbitration agreement. The parties can contract to submit disputes to a panel of experts outside the market country. International arbitration panels currently exist, either set up by markets or independently run, and could be used to resolve disputes exported from countries where judicial corruption is perceived as a problem.

There are several levels at which foreign dispute resolution works now, and can be expanded to counteract problems such as local corruption. First, the place where judicial resolution is sought must permit its tribunals to take jurisdiction over cases which arose abroad. Most modern legal systems make provision for this. They vary regarding the extent of the scope of their international jurisdiction,[13] but

12. For example, in the sense that those favoured by the corrupt may be allowed to conduct business more cheaply than those not so favoured, or that they may be given favourable results in dispute settlements which require those not bribing officials to pay money to those that do pay such bribes.

13. For example, it is generally conceded that the US has a far broader view of the scope of the international jurisdiction of its courts than most other countries, including the UK.

permit some classes of foreign cases to be tried in their courts. A decision by market centres to export disputes for foreign resolution requires different kinds of agreement. It is by no means clear that any government would permit its judicial system to be used for dispute resolution by a foreign country, because, among many other things, the increased costs of the additional cases would be a burden on the taxpayers. However, there are ways around this problem. A country with a highly regarded judicial system could make a decision to its judicial forums available for a fee, perhaps calculated as a percentage of the market business. This could be done either by opening ordinary commercial courts to the market nation's cases, or by establishing separate, although government supervised, courts available for that purpose. This would permit both governments to earn revenue from the market business, and would reduce traders' overall costs by diminishing the 'tax' of corruption in the market nation.

The other solution is to export dispute resolution to non-government arbitration panels of experts in other locations. It may well be sensible for these panels to be jointly subsidised by the market centre governments, and by the trade itself. The governments would benefit from the impartial dispute resolution provided, and the trade would benefit from that and from increased business in a new market.

In respect of both export to government, or private, tribunals there are some procedural problems to be considered which are raised by such things as distance and differences of language. However, there are international tribunals operating now which deal with cases in several languages and language differences, although they add to cost, can be overcome. Many problems having to do with distance can be solved by having much of the dispute, and perhaps all of certain disputes, decided on written submissions.

Enforcement of any such decisions is another issue. In the event that market place government would co-operate in enforcement of foreign decisions, awards can probably be collected. Alternatively, awards may be able to be enforced in foreign jurisdictions where assets of the losing party are located.

### 4.3.2 Clearing and delivery

Dispute resolution is not the only market-related function that can be exported. Clearing, that is the matching of buy and sell orders together with account crediting and debiting, can be performed by computer at distant locations. Delivery of commodities can also be performed overseas, indeed, at the New York Coffee, Sugar & Cocoa Exchange delivery on certain sugar contracts (No.11 Sugar) must be made abroad.

The point of this is to show that certain costs associated with trading in a particular market can be reduced by exporting them to locations where they can be done more efficiently, thus reducing the overall transaction costs to traders in the market. Government regulators can use this device to gain competitive advantages for their markets.

Instant communications and easy electronic transfer of funds around the globe means the various components that constitute a futures market can be separated, and performed in places where it is more economical, even if those places are widely separated. This has two significant market consequences. First, if a particular market component is particularly costly in any market location, it can be exported to a place where it can be performed more cheaply. This reduces transaction costs to the traders, and makes the market's continued existence more viable. The market's continuation keeps it a revenue producing enterprise for the country in which it is located. Secondly, the possibility of exporting certain functions to reduce costs, allows market locations to remain competitive with other potential market locations, and diminish the risks that all of a market's business will move abroad in order to benefit from a reduced cost structure.

## 5. EXAMINATION OF THE PRACTICAL EFFECTS OF REGULATION

Having made some examination of the types and methods of regulation, it is important to explore how they interact with other factors to influence the location of futures and derivatives markets, both in the present and in the past.

## 5.1 Theories of international trade

### 5.1.1 Traditional trade theory

Under traditional economic theory, which held sway until the 1980s, international trade was usually seen in terms of commodities, such as wheat, oil, and rubber.[14] It was said that differences in countries gave them the abilities to produce different commodities, and international trade occurred to take advantage of those differences.

Under such a theory, the derivatives trade occurs in London because that city possesses inherent differences which make it a natural place to centre such trade. In line with this theory, certain advantages of the London markets are often cited such as: location between American and Far Eastern time zones, a tradition of financial trading, the tradition of English common law, the English language, and a historical relationship with US markets. However, an important drawback in this point of view is that it lulls adherents into thinking that the advantages of London are so established that there is no serious danger that the trade will move elsewhere. Such smugness may be encouraged in the present trading climate where US market share of the financial services business is declining, with such business being attracted to Europe in general, and London in particular. Any complacency about the reasons why financial services markets are successful in London is particularly dangerous in a country such as the United Kingdom which has one-fifth of its GNP produced by invisible trade, about half of which is produced the financial services business. Indeed, the United Kingdom is more dependant on invisibles than any other G7 nation.[15]

14. Paul R. Krugman, *Rethinking International Trade* (Cambridge, MA: MIT Press, 1990), pp. 1–3.
15. British Invisibles, *Annual Report & Accounts 1992* (London, 1992), pp. 18–20.

### 5.1.2 New international trade theory

In the 1980s a new theory of international trade was evolved by a group of economists led by Paul R. Krugman of MIT. It is his view that differences between countries are only one reason for international trade. The other important reason, is the advantages of specialisation.

Economies of scale offer advantages that focus trade in a few, relatively efficient market centres. In futures and derivatives, specialisation offers increasing returns that lead to the business becoming focused in places such as London.

This theory supports a belief that economies of scale will keep the business in major market centres such as London, and, indeed, will promote its continued growth, at the expense of smaller financial centres.[16] However, such a conclusion is also dangerous for England in that it promotes complacency of the kind mentioned above, and tells little about the loss of business being experienced by the United States, or the growth of the Paris MATIF, and Frankfurt's DTB.

In the context of competition for futures and derivatives markets an important factor that also has to be considered is the availability of freedom of contract. National differences matter. Economies of scale matter. But discussion of their influences on trade describe only part of the issue. It can be argued that the key determinant to the location of trade in derivatives is the availability of freedom to contract.

### 5.1.3 Freedom to contract

At this point some clarification of terms is in order. Availability of freedom to contract not the same as free, or unregulated trade. On the contrary, the availability of freedom of contract can be assured only by vigilant and judicious regulation. First, regulatory laws must be formulated so as to extend freedom of contract in ways that often

16. E.P. Davis, *International Financial Centres – An Industrial Analysis*, (London: Bank of England, 1990), p. 15.

go beyond existing laws, and cultural and historical traditions. Secondly, in order to maximise the benefits of derivatives business, markets and their regulations must be monitored and adjusted to continually assure that they are not being abused to commit fraud on customers or to prevent the market entry of new, and hopefully innovative and more efficient, competitors.

Judicious regulation is an important tool for preserving the vitality of important derivatives markets. The absence of effective regulation, just as much as the existence of oppressive regulation, can cause financial market business to grow elsewhere.

Ultimately, the availability of freedom of contract is a function of: (a) regulation, and (b) its cost. Cost of freedom of contract is sum total that must be paid to overcome the barriers to obtaining its benefits. This cost can have many components such as those discussed in 4.1 above.

The components of cost are so numerous that it is difficult to be able to list all of them for any market. However, it is possible for a regulator to judge whether an addition to regulation will add to the costs of entering into derivatives contracts within his jurisdiction. This perception has to be balanced against judgment as to whether the regulation decreases costs to majority of traders, *ie*, reduces barriers to market entry or decreases opportunities for fraud and market manipulation. Is the regulation one which is needed to maintain market confidence? This is a question that is often asked when considering tighter market regulation, but on the other hand, it is extremely difficult to know how the potential level of market confidence measured.

The basic question that regulator must ask itself is: are regulations adding costs to entering into these contracts which are not present in competing markets, creating a danger that sectors of the business may move to less restricted jurisdictions? If costs are being added, are they balanced in some reasonably measurable respect, so that the regulator can make a reasonable judgment about whether he is likely to be driving the business abroad?

## 5.2 What has determined location in past?

There is evidence that the costs imposed by regulation were important in determining where markets were located.

One aspect of this as it bears on present thinking about expansion of derivative instrument trading to developing or newly emerging nations is the belief, that derivative contracts are difficult to introduce into states that are unfamiliar with principles of English (and now, Anglo-American) common law, because the historical foundations of derivative contracts are found in the common law.

Nonsense! The idea of recognising the legitimacy of a consensual contract for future delivery is wholly alien to the fundamental principles of English common law. The idea that one could have a valid contract which consists of the parties consenting to some future performance came very late to English law. Until about the thirteenth century, executory contracts were not enforceable under English common law because under the doctrine of seisin, followed there, the rights to a thing were not separable from the thing itself. Property rights went with possession. Also, determination of disputes depended on supernatural interventions in such things as trial by ordeal, or trial by combat, which were no way to conduct a business and could make the cost insupportably high. It was not until the seventeenth century the English law adopted the legal principals necessary to find that contracts for future delivery were enforceable, and assignable to others. That was the beginning of contract markets, in futures and derivatives, in England.

The contract principals which are the basis of the United Kingdom and United States modern futures and derivative markets were borrowed from Roman law, long used by church and mercantile courts for settling commercial disputes. Roman law, at least as restated in the time of Justinian's *Corpus Juris* recognised the validity of a wide variety of derivative contracts, and their assignability. However, the principals of Roman contract law which are the basis of modern futures and derivatives contracts did not originate in Rome, but in ancient Mesopotamia.

In the collection of the British Museum there is a

cuneiform tablet, dating from about 1750 BC, which translates as follows:[17]

> 204 2/3 qu of oil in the measure of Shamash, to the value of 1/3 mina 2/3 shekels of silver, as the price of healthy slaves from Gutium, Warad-Marduk son of Ibni-Marduk has received from Utul-Ishtar the troop-commander on the authority of Lu-Ishurra son of Ili-usati. Within one month he shall bring healthy slaves from Gutium. If he does not bring them within one month, Lu-Ishkurra son of Ili-usati will repay 1/3 mina 2/3 shekels of silver to the bearer of his tablet.
> Before Ilshu-ibni son of Sin-eribam.
> Before Iluna son of Ipqusha.
> Before Belshunu son of Ilshu-bani.
> Before Ipqatum son of Taribum.
> Month Ab, 6th day, year in which King Ammisaduqa, the faithful obedient shepherd of Shamash and Marduk, etc.

This is just one of many examples of contracts of future delivery, usually following this form, that have been unearthed in Mesopotamia, from 2000 BC. onwards. Why did derivatives trading originate there? There seem to have been two reasons: practical necessity, and legal regulation.

### 5.2.1 Practical necessity

As far as is known, the region of Mesopotamia was the site of the first organised agricultural production of commodities such as grains. Regular food supply, and surpluses created by these agricultural advances, led to permitted the growth of city-states, where populations of more specialised workers lived and traded. This was the dominant political unit of Mesopotamian culture.

Eventually, the populations of these city-states outgrew the capacity of local agricultural producers to guarantee their food supply, and conquest of other food-producing areas was often impractical because of relative balance of military power, or because of desire to avoid the problems of war. A new method was required to gain control of needed commodity supplies. There are no known documents

17. Dr. Christopher Walker of the British Museum.

describing how it was decided to adopt contracts for future delivery as trading devices, or why it was decided that such contracts could be assignable to third parties, but there is no question that the use of such contracts gave an important advantage to those cultures that used them over competitors for supplies of foodstuffs, and other commodities.

That advantage was that buyers who had the opportunity to use such contracts were in a position to offer firm commitments, not merely to buy commodities available on the spot, to buy future supplies. Derivative instruments gave them a significant measure of control over quantities of grain, that purely 'spot-trading' cultures could not match. Consequently, these early derivative instruments were a revolutionary path to control and power over the marketing and distribution of vital commodities in the ancient Near East.

### 5.2.2 Regulation

The ancient cuneiform contract quoted above tells a great deal about how its form gave its users a competitive advantage by lowering the costs of the derivatives business.

First, it is a written contract. This makes determination of the terms much more certain than relying on memories affected by the passage of time, and changes of circumstances.

Secondly, it was is in standard form, drawn by professionally trained scribes. The use of a recognised standard form diminished misunderstandings about the purpose and meaning of the contract.

The names of witness are included. This, together with independent legal writings such as the contemporaneous, Code of Hammurabi, King of Babylon, show that legal regulations permitted proof of contracts supported by the written evidence, and the testimony of witnesses. No supernatural intervention is required, unlike cases in early English common law, or other early European codes of law. There seems little doubt that producing written documents and witnesses was a far cheaper method of proving the terms of a contract, than obtaining a credible pronouncement from the relevant god.

A wide latitude in permitting the use of derivative instruments is shown by this contract. This is not merely inferred because items promised for future delivery are slaves. The seller is permitted to deliver either slaves or an amount of silver. The seller to had the option of choosing the least expensive of two alternatives, and saved the cost of proving the amount of damages if he failed to deliver the slaves.

Finally, this contract is in fact a bearer bond. By its terms, the contract was assignable to anyone, without any additional costs having to be incurred by formally modifying the contract. As far as is known there were no regulatory restrictions as to who could use such contracts, where or when such transactions had to be performed, or what commodities could be sold.

Thus, at the very beginning of the derivatives business we see the critical elements of liberal scope for freedom of contracts, at comparatively low cost. There can be little doubt that the ancient society that drew this contract found it a powerful economic tool. How could neighbouring societies without written contracts, and relying on the supernatural settlement of disputes, have competed commercially?

The control of commodities and trading flexibility given by these derivatives contracts was noticed by the neighbours and trading partners of the Mesopotamian city states, because historical analysis research shows that these forms of doing business eventually migrated from Mesopotamia, with the cuneiform writing, to the shores of the Mediterranean, down to Egypt, where they were continued by the Hellenistic empires of the successors of Alexander the Great. They began to influence changes in Roman Law about 200 BC (when Rome needed to traded with Egypt and Syria to assure its own food supplies). The commodity control and market power conferred by futures contracts was observed and appreciated by Rome which incorporated consensual contracts for future commodities (*res futurae*) into its own commercial law. Through the legacy of Roman law, derivative instruments have become part of modern commerce in developed countries. Roman commercial contract law was preserved in the laws of Constantinople and the post-Roman Italian trading cities, such as Venice, Amalfi, Pisa and

Genoa. Italian city states continued trading in the eastern Mediterranean before and after the Crusades, and brought Roman commercial law to the medieval fairs of Champagne, and the European centres Bruges, Antwerp, Amsterdam. From those market cities, it migrated to London and from there to the United States and Japan.

It is not appropriate here to cover the entire fascinating historical journey from Mesopotamia to London but this brief look gives some insight into the economic power that was conferred by legal regulation of derivatives, even in the most ancient times.[18]

## 5.3 Determination of market location today

It is very hard to know the actual value of futures contracts and other derivative instruments traded worldwide on an annual bases. Statistics vary widely. However, all observers agree that the number is large and increasing. Some recent statistics state that the value of exchange-traded futures worldwide is about US$140 trillion (US$140,000 billion) annually.[19] The outstanding value of swaps between banks is about US$4.5 trillion.[20] The face value of derivative-driven foreign exchange contracts may, according to recent figures given out by the New York Federal Reserve bank, probably exceed US$300,000 billion annually. Of foreign exchange transactions, more than half is derivative instruments such as forward contracts or swaps.[21] Consequently, the total of derivative instrument-driven transactions may be around the astronomical sum of US$500,000 billion annually.

Clearly, this is a business worth competing for. The

18. For a more complete summary of the historical evolution of this trade see, Edward J. Swan, *The Development of the Law of Financial Services* (London: Cavendish, 1993), chapters 1–3.

19. Tracy Corrigan, 'Quirky Offshoots Gain Respect', *Financial Times* (London: 20 Oct. 1993), Survey, Section III, p. 6; and David Waller, 'Bundesbank says derivatives pose threat to world markets', Financial Times, Section I, p. 1.

20. Ibid.

21. Bank for International Settlements, *Central Bank Survey of Foreign Exchange Market Activity in April 1992* (Basle: March 1993), p. 6.

competition for this futures and derivatives business is now largely seen as being between the well-established relatively flexible markets in London; the huge but traditionally more exchange-trading orientated markets of the United States; the newly competitive markets of Germany, France, and other states in Europe; and the markets of the Far East.

For the United States, otherwise the world's largest economy, the competition is not going well. Between 1989 and 1992, the United States already a distant second to the United Kingdom as a market for foreign exchange transactions saw its market share shrink slightly, while the UK's increased.[22] In less than ten years, US futures exchanges have seen their market share of the world's futures contracts shrink from around 95 per cent to less than 65 per cent.[23] *The International Herald Tribune* reported it to be less than 50 per cent in November 1992.[24] In London, market share almost doubled in the same period. In 1993, business on London's LIFFE was about 20 per cent higher than in 1992, and at the Paris MATIF about 30 per cent higher.[25]

In the United States there have been significant increases in the trading volume of some exchanges: notably the Chicago Mercantile Exchange and the Chicago Board of Trade.[26] However, there is concern that the United States is bleeding business to London and Europe, and that its markets are losing the competition for the huge and increasingly important derivatives business. To the extent that this is happening, it can hardly be said to be the result of inherent differences between countries, or because of economies of scale. Commodities exchanges, trading in futures contracts, have existed since before the American Revolution, and a large proportion of the world's trade in derivative instruments is conducted there. A key reason why US markets have difficulty competing for derivative instrument business is that,

22. Id., 14.

23. E.P. Davis, *International Financial Centres – an Industrial Analysis*, Bank of England Discussion Papers, No. 91 (Sept. 1990), p. 18.

24. Barnaby J. Feder, 'Chicago Challenge: Secure the Futures', *International Herald Tribune* (London: 30 Nov. 1992), p. 24.

25. 'Derive and Rule', *The Economist* (London: 7 Aug. 1993), p. 73.

26. *Financial Times*, Section III, p. 6.

when compared with competing jurisdictions, freedom to enter into derivative instruments is tightly restricted, and the present regulatory structure makes the cost of entering into these contracts relatively high.

Since the American Revolution, the individual states have restricted the right to enter into derivative instrument contracts in various ways. Since 1922, the Federal government has restricted freedom of contract in derivatives, by making a fundamental principle of US trading that futures contracts can be entered into only on authorised exchanges. This restriction on trade venues adds to the costs of dealing in such contracts in a number of ways, such as requiring that such transactions can be executed only through exchange members who must be paid a fee to help them profit from their high-priced purchases of exchange memberships (called 'seats').

A recent study of what motivates companies to locate financial services business in a particular market centre has concluded that costs of transacting that business is a key factor.[27] In order for a firm to obtain the right to undertake derivatives business in the United States there are so many levels of regulation, so many overlapping legal restrictions, and so many registration and reporting requirements that it is very difficult to calculate the costs of entering the derivatives business. However, some recent observations have been made.

In March 1993, the Corporation of London published a City Research Project by the London Business School on *The Costs and Effectiveness of the UK Financial Regulatory System*. That report compared the relative costs, to financial services firms, of doing business in the United States, the United Kingdom and France. It concluded that in securities and derivatives trading and broking, 'UK costs do appear clearly lower than those of US securities and derivatives trading and broking. .'.[28] Their attempts to quantify the

27. Julian Franks and Stephen Shaffer, *The Costs and Effectiveness of the UK Financial Regulating System* (London, London Business School, Mar. 1993).
28. Id., p. 21.

reasons for this conclusion show the following:

(1) The US has eight major regulatory bodies (excluding smaller exchanges and state regulators), whereas the UK has four.[29]

(2) The UK has between 5 and 7 regulators per 1000 people working in the industry, whereas the US has nearly 12.[30]

(3) The cost of regulation, born by industry, is between in between \$150–\$500 less per industry employee in the UK than it is in the US.[31]

Recently, the United States has made some attempts to make its markets more competitive. In 1992 the Futures Trading Practices Act[32] was passed by Congress which allows the Commodity Futures Trading Commission ('CFTC') to exempt from regulation any derivatives trading which meets certain tests, including preventing fraud and protecting market integrity, where the Commission concludes the transactions are entered into by appropriate persons such as institutional or professional traders.[33] A swaps exemption from Commodity Exchange Act ('CEA') regulation was approved by the CFTC in January 1993, although the authority to investigate claims of fraud was retained. Certain hybrid instruments were also exempted from the CEA regulation. In April 1993, an energy products exemption for trading of contracts between 'appropriate persons' was established.[34]

It can certainly be argued that this new policy of exempting certain markets from regulation will encourage established traders in certain sectors of the derivative instrument business to do more trading in the United States, because of the freedom from certain kinds of regulation that these new exemptions give. However, it can also be argued that this new

29. Id., p. 19.
30. Id., p. 24.
31. Id., p. 24.
32. Pub. L. 102–546, 106 Stat. 3590 (1992).
33. Commodity Exchange Act section 4(c)(2)(B), 7 U.S.C., section 6(c)(2)(B) (1992).
34. 58 Fed. Reg. 21236 at 21294 (20 Apr. 1993).

power to grant exemptions to certain derivative markets makes access to freedom to contract derivative instruments more complex and costly. Essentially, this policy divides traders into two groups: those subject to Commodity Exchange Act regulation, which applies to the general population of merchants; and those affluent enough to pay the heavy legal costs of applying for, and are fortunate enough to obtain, an exemption for their particular kind of trading.

In those markets that are exempt, it can be argued that the government is abdicating its important regulatory function of encouraging and promoting the healthy growth of the derivatives business by leaving such issues of market access, fraud and market manipulation in the entirely self-interested hands of the present market members. It seems very likely that such a situation could eventually lead to the sclerosis of these derivatives markets in the United States. While there may be some short term gains, in the long-run such a policy will continue to drive US derivatives business overseas, where freedom to contract derivatives instruments is easier and cheaper to obtain, and protected by judicious regulation.

# 6. FUTURE COMPETITION FOR DERIVATIVES MARKETS

In the future it seems very likely that derivatives business will go to those jurisdictions that are able to keep in focus the concept that the product they are offering to the commercial world is freedom to contract, and their market share will be determined by how much it costs.

This could present an opportunity for developing nations to expand their economies. The bigger the derivatives business gets, the more opportunities there should be to compete profitably for different aspects of the business. The increasing speed of international communication and transportation continually makes it more feasible to locate different components of the derivatives business in different geographical locations.

The option of being able to export particular components of futures market trading, or its support functions (as discussed in section 4.3, above), is an aspect of modern market trading which can be described as the 'commoditisation' of futures markets. This refers to the fact that, as the markets grow in the modern international trading environment, each component service which contributes to the market becomes a commodity which can be a subject of competition between competing service providers and competing market centres.

Increasing commoditisation may develop as the markets grow. This is a different way of looking at market growth. A common view is that one result of market growth will be increasing centralisation. The thought is that services of the kind used by futures markets can be more efficiently provided in a single central location, such as the City and Docklands of London. In the abstract, this view has some appeal. Taking London as an example, there are a number of attractions that can be cited as reasons why it is a good place to centralise the futures business. These include: London's history of having been a central market for futures, its cultural ties with the markets of America, its historical ties with many important commodity producing nations, its convenient time zone location between North America and the Far East, a respected legal system, relatively streamlined regulation, political stability, modern communications facilities, proximity to continental Europe, and the use of the English language.

However, it would be a competitive error to believe that any of these, or all of them together, will guarantee London's continued prominence as a futures trading centre. It can be argued that there is no inherent virtue in any of these things. Their competitive significance derives from the fact that, taken singly and together, they make London a less expensive jurisdiction than competing market centres in which to do business. As the size of the business grows, rather than consolidating London's position as a market centre, the growth may stimulate loss of market share. As the size of the futures trading markets grow, more revenue will be generated by each component of the market and the services that support it. Consequently, opportunities for profit will increase. This will provide incentives for increased competition between different parties, and indeed different market centres, to acquire the business of those individual components. This increased competition may attract different market functions to different market centres to the extent that it makes it loss costly to perform those functions in other locations. Market growth, rather than leading to increasing centralisation, is a force for decentralisation by promoting competition for efficiency.

## 6.1 The impact of commoditisation on regulation

In general, such competition will improve the efficiency of the markets, lower their transaction costs and make their benefits available to a wider constituency. By dividing markets into their components and offering the business of performing the functions of those components to a wider pool of bidders, the costs of performing those functions will increasingly be a better reflection of their value. More potential buyers will provide better price competition.

In regulatory terms the commoditisation of market components has important implications. Regulatory schemes to date have tended to view futures markets as consisting of an indivisible body of unique components, principally centred in a single jurisdiction, that can best be regulated by a single comprehensive regulatory philosophy. The growth of the futures business is leading to increasing internationalisation, with different, but related products being sold in different jurisdictions, by a variety of organisations, including the interrelated components of multinationals. Consequently, if regulation is in fact used as a form of 'interference' (as discussed in section 2, above) in the markets, the lure of greater profits is an incentive for the futures business to move to markets where there is less interference.

This movement has historically been observed as a reaction to government regulation in a number of markets. The result is that the debate about what form regulation should take has come to be viewed as a choice between more or less regulation. One camp is of the view that less regulation, often called 'free trade', is the way to promote market growth; as opposed to regulatory 'interference' which is said to drive business away by making local markets 'less competitive'. Others promote the view that restrictive regulation is necessary to prevent 'fraud' or other market failures, such as the insolvency of major traders which harm the public. There are elements of truth in each of these views, but neither is the most productive method of accomplishing what are claimed to be its goals. Unregulated trade leaves the business at the mercy of those with the greatest market power, who can use that power to restrict supply, raise prices, and inhibit the market entry of others. Restrictive regulation will never be adequate to prevent the invention of new frauds or the assumption of unacceptable risks, because the avenues of business change too rapidly for any system of regulation to adjust quickly enough.

Consequently, it would not take very sophisticated changes in either the legal systems or the market facilities of Third World and newly emerging nations for them to be able to perform some components of the derivatives business much more cheaply than they are being performed in established markets. It takes only a modest change of mind for their regulators to start competing for, and winning portions of the derivatives business, which may well grow substantially in the future.

In order to assure that markets remain healthy, both regulators and the regulated must co-operate to obtain judicious regulation that will promote freedom to contract at a reasonable price. Absence of regulation, in the international derivatives markets is no answer, because in international markets competitors have different national tax and regulatory advantages and handicaps. Merchants are not competing equally in the international business of derivatives, and lack of regulation will only emphasise such inequalities.

Regulation is necessary to try to make the trading conditions fair and honest. Responsibility must not be abdicated by regulatory bodies. Nor must traders neglect to insist on sensible regulation, because if they do, they are ng an advantage to their competitors which may well damage the market by leading to diminished competition.

# 7. CONCLUSION: REGULATION AS MARKET PARTICIPATION

In any market, the regulating government has an opportunity to increase or decrease the economic benefits realised by society as a whole by the existence of the market. This gives the regulating jurisdiction a stake in the market. In such circumstances, it is not very useful to see regulation as a matter of 'interference' in the market. The true interest of the regulator is one of 'participation' in the sense that the regulating government is a partner of the trading community in the conduct of the market. Their interests are on a continuum. The actions of each in the market effect the other. To view the interests of the regulator and the regulated as being necessarily at odds oversimplifies the issue of regulation. The prosperity of the traders is not the central issue on the question of whether to regulate or not to regulate. The central issue is how to regulate the markets so that a favourable balance is struck between the interests of the traders and the interests of the regulating society as a whole.

Complex international market systems, such as the type in which futures are traded, require a more sensitive policy of government regulation than observation of closed, single nation economic systems would suggest. A policy to encourage the growth and prosperity of such markets is not necessarily best-served by a decision to reduce and eliminate regulation. The prosperity of complex international futures trade may best be promoted by thorough, but sensitive government regulation of several factors which affect the functioning of the markets. These include, the degree of freedom of contract, specific regulation of financial services, tax, currency controls, import/export restrictions, and immigration laws. Sensitive government regulation of each of these seemingly separate areas contributes to the growth and prosperity of futures markets. Whether a government wishes to discourage or encourage the growth of futures markets within its borders, it is in partnership with, rather than separate from, commercial interests.

The key element in the partnership is the law of contract. This determines whether the business will exist at all. At the very least, a regulatory jurisdiction must have a contract law that recognises the validity of consensual contracts to deliver commodities in the future. Such a contract law expands the scope of the economic power of the merchants trading under it to a whole new range of previously untradeable commodities. Similarly, the recognition of such contracts brings that range of commodities within the power of the government in the sense that it may benefit, in taxes or other ways, from the revenues generated by trading those previously unavailable commodities. The regulating government also may exercise power over who may trade in such future commodities and under what circumstances.

Immigration policy is also a market entry policy in that it determines who, and for what reasons, people may enter and remain in the regulating jurisdiction. Import/export controls affect what may be traded within the country and under what circumstances. Currency controls affect terms of payment and taxes affect the profitability of the trade. In general, each of these things, and a substantial list of others that could be added make it more or less difficult to engage in the futures business. The carefully thought out regulatory participation of the government is needed to arrange these impinging factors in the manner best calculated to encourage those aspects of futures market trade which the government wishes to encourage and to discourage those things which it wishes to prevent. Given the complexity of international trade in futures and the many factors which determine its profitability, it is not accurate, or even possible, to think of regulation of this business in terms of 'restrictive' or 'hands-off' regulation. Such thoughts focus on the far too narrow view of the futures business being a discrete enterprise that is best regulated with specialised, purpose-drawn regulations to fine tune it. To try and do that is to be blind to the nature of the business as a worldwide network of interrelated contracts encompassing a wide range of financial transactions. What is really needed is thoughtful, participatory regulation designed to expand government control over the economic benefits generated by the business without driving away the trade that creates them.[35]

35. W. Brian Arthur, 'Pandora's Marketplace', *New Scientist*, supplement (6 Feb. 1993), pp. 6–8, 7.

*Chapter 8*

# MATHEMATICAL MODELLING OF DERIVATIVES MARKETS

Professor D.D. Vvedensky,
Imperial College, London

## 1. INTRODUCTION AND BACKGROUND

The movement of derivatives markets presents a considerable challenge to the mathematical modeller. The complexity and richness exhibited by the activity of these markets bears the signatures of non-linear and non-equilibrium behaviour that is also a feature of many physical and mathematical models. Not surprisingly, therefore, many of the methods used for modelling these latter systems have also found fertile ground for applications in derivative markets and other financial settings. However, unlike physical and mathematical models, where data can be collected under various conditions and often in whatever quantity desired, data on markets is extremely limited. This has often acted as an inhibiting factor in the unambiguous interpretation of market behaviour in terms of specific models. Nevertheless, the casting of market behaviour within a mathematical framework does open up a wealth of analytic machinery that has been thoroughly tested by scientists, engineers, mathematicians and statisticians.

There are several ways in which mathematical modelling can provide useful information about movements in financial markets. The construction of a model underscores the fundamental assumptions and beliefs about the behaviour of markets and how the markets can be influenced. An examination of these assumptions is crucial to an understanding and assessment of the risks involved in investing in a

131

particular financial instrument. There is also the question of the effect of policy changes on market activity. For derivatives markets in particular, where global policies on several issues are still being developed, a model could show whether particular policy changes inhibit, promote, or leave unaffected the behaviour of the market. The treasury model of the UK economy is an example where a mathematical model, based on certain assumptions regarding the economy and its mathematical realisation, has been used to influence policy by solving the model under different conditions.

This chapter will review the most frequently used mathematical methods for modelling derivatives markets, focussing on stochastic equations, computer simulation, and the dynamics of chaotic systems. The emphasis will be on the practical application of the methods and on the type of information that can be obtained with each approach.

The outline of this chapter is as follows. In Section 2, I will identify the features of the market that are regarded as the most important for developing quantitative models. Some aspects of financial markets can be readily identified, but others, such as the *source* of the irregular movements of prices, are still a matter of some debate. The survey of mathematical methods will begin in Section 3, with the simplest random process, the so-called random walk, which is in essence a coin toss experiment. This type of randomness is the basis of many studies in the physical and mathematical sciences, if only as a limiting case for the behaviour of real systems. The 'normal' distribution will be derived from this process and its relation to the assumptions used to model market movements will be clarified. Modifications of the random walk process will be described in Section 4. The Black-Scholes model of option pricing – perhaps the best-known example of mathematical modelling of derivatives markets – will be covered in this section. In Section 5, a different approach to analysing market movements will be described. These techniques have been spawned out of work carried out in the past 15 years on systems that exhibit what has come to be known as chaotic behaviour. I will focus on methods of data analysis that reveal some quite unexpected features of market movements which challenge some of the long-held assumptions of their behaviour. A summary of the methods covered in this chapter together with outstanding issues is in Section 6.

# 2. CHARACTERISING THE MARKET

There are several questions that must be addressed in attempting to model any system. Broadly speaking, the most important of these are as follows. Is the system in equilibrium? In the most general terms an equilibrium system is one which is 'at rest', *ie*, the properties of the system do not change with time and the system is not exchanging any quantity with its environment. Thus, a sealed bottle of water is an equilibrium system, but a reservoir is not, since it accrues water from an adjacent lake and water is drained from the reservoir to prevent overflowing. Any financial market (investors, brokers, traders, etc.) must be regarded as being a *non-equilibrium* system because the quantity being acquired is information which, in turn, is translated into the behaviour of the market process of, say, a derivative instrument, a stock, or a collective indicator of a Stock Exchange.

Two additional important characteristics that must be identified are the behaviour of parts of the system in relation to one another. In particular, do these parts behave independently or is there some co-operation or correlations among the parts. In market terms, these 'parts' are individual or groups of investors, traders, etc. The behaviour of these parts relate both to whether the market behaves *linearly* or *non-linearly* and if the market is predictable or if there is an element of randomness in its movement. Financial markets show behaviour that is both non-linear and unpredictable. The behaviour is unpredictable because different investors respond in different ways to the same situation. But they do not necessarily behave *independently*. The unpredictability means that values of, say, a stock option, are described by a distribution of possible values together with their likelihoods rather than by a single number. This, in turn, implies that there is an uncertainty in the values of the stock, the magnitude of which is called the *volatility* of the stock.

A question closely related to randomness is the *memory* of the system. This is best shown in the context of an example. The successive flipping of a coin or spinning of a roulette wheel are independent events in the sense that the result obtained from any particular trial (flipping or spining) is independent of preceding results. Such a random process is called *Markovian*. A Markovian process retains no memory of its history. An example of a non-Markovian process is drawing cards of an imperfectly shuffled pack of cards. There will be sequences of cards that reflect the memory of originally being arranged in a particular order. Financial markets cannot be expected to Markovian for the reasons that the investors do not disregard previous information and they do not act independently. A slightly more subtle effect is related to how completely information is distributed to investors.

A final question is one that has arisen only in recent years and relates to the *origin* of the unpredictability of a system, *ie*, whether it is true randomness or whether there is an underlying order to the apparently erratic behaviour of such a system. This is closely related to a field that has been given the name of 'chaos' (Gleich, 1987). In terms of financial analysis, the techniques used to analyse such systems can used to ascertain issues concerning the memory of the system, whether the system is expected to exhibit chaos, and whether a new approach to modelling is required. Needless to say, the use of such ideas has led to a critical examination of many long-held notions in the analysis of financial markets, but there are still much work to be done in this rapidly-developing area.

## 3. THE RANDOM WALK AND THE EFFICIENT MARKET HYPOTHESIS

The random walk is the simplest random process and has been used as a starting point to describe many physical phenomena involving an element of randomness. It is also sometimes referred to as a *Weiner process* after the mathematician Norbert Weiner who developed many of the mathematical methods used to study such processes in the 1920s. An example of a random walk is the cumulative result of successive tosses of a coin. Consider the following experiment. Toss a coin and record whether the coins lands face up ('heads') or face down ('tails'). A quantity $s$ is defined that records the numbers of heads and tails in the following way. For every toss that yields heads, add one to the total values of $s$ and for every toss that yields 'tails', add minus one to this total. The initial value of $s$ is zero. Thus, the sum at the end of a given number of tries is the number of additional heads in excess of tails (if the sum is positive) or the number of tails in excess of heads (if the sum is negative). The term 'random walk' refers to the fact that if a point is moved one position to the right (resp., left) for every result of heads (resp., tails) the point executes a 'walk', with the sum representing the net movement of the point to the right or to the left from the starting position.

This example illustrate two important points. The first concerns the randomness of the process. The result of a coin toss is considered to be random because the force imparted to the coin as it is tossed in the air has not been calculated. If that information had been available it would be possible to *calculate* the result of any toss. In this regard, the randomness is related to the limited information about the coin toss. (In Section 5 I will consider a cause of randomness that is intrinsic to the system, *ie,* not due to a lack of information). The second point concerns the result of tossing a coin $N$ times ($N = 1, 2, \ldots$). Because of the randomness of the system, there will be a *distribution* of possible results. In other words, if two sequences of $N$ tosses are performed it is likely to achieve two different values of $s$. Consider two sequences of 20 tosses of the coin, and signify a result of heads by '$H$' and as result of tails by '$T$'.

Example (1)

Sequence 1: *HHHTTHTHTTTHTTHHTTTT*
Sequence 2: *HHTHTTTHTTHHHHTTTHHT*

In the first sequence there are eight heads and 12 tails, while in the second sequence, ten heads and ten tails. Thus, the values of $s$ for these two sequences is $s = 8 - 12 = -4$ for the first sequence and $s = 10 - 10 = 0$ for the second sequence, indicating that there is a net movement of four steps to the left during the first sequence, but no net movement during the second sequence. Figure 1 shows the behaviour of $s$ for three sequences of 1000 tosses of a coin. There are several common features to the three sequences, including the erratic paths taken by $s$ and the absence of any discernible pattern to the paths. Notice also the markedly different paths taken by $s$, showing relatively large deviations both to the left and to the right. The likelihood of such large deviations increases as the number of trials increases, as I will discuss below.

As the number of sequences is increased, the frequency of a particular value is given by a function called $P(s)$, that has the following form:

Example (2)

$$ P(s) = \frac{1}{\sqrt{2\pi\sigma^2}} \exp\left[ -\frac{(s-u)^2}{2\sigma^2} \right] $$

This distribution is called the 'Gaussian' or 'normal' distribution. The latter name indicates just how important and common this distribution is in the analysis of random processes. The normal distribution contains two quantities, $\mu$ and $\sigma$, that completely characterise this distribution. The quantity $\mu$ is the *mean*, or *average* of the distribution. The quantity $\mu^2$ is called the *variance* and the $\sigma$ is called the *root-mean-square* (rms) deviation or the *standard deviation*, with the latter providing a measure of the width of the distribution, or the 'spread' in the outcomes of trials from the distribution. In market terms, $\sigma$ represents the volatility of the quantity being measured, eg. stocks, bonds or other financial instruments.

The values of $\mu$ and $\sigma$ for the coin toss model of the random walk after $N$ coin tosses are

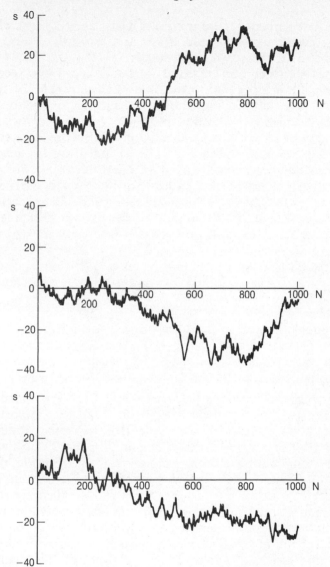

**Figure 1** The behaviour of a random walk during three sequences of 1000 coin tosses. The position of the 'walker' at any time with respect to the horizontal line represents the difference between the numbers of heads and tails up to that point. When the position is above (resp., below) the line, the number of heads, or positive steps, is greater (resp., less) than the number of tails, or negative steps.

Example (3)

$$\mu = 0, \qquad \sigma = \sqrt{N}$$

The average value of $s$ being zero means that on average the number of heads is equal to the number of tails. This is to be expected since the likelihood of a coin toss producing heads or tails. The second equation in (3) states that the variance ($\sigma^2$) increases in direct proportion (linearly) with the number of coin tosses $N$. In other words, the likelihood of finding a large deviation to the right or to the left in a random walk (respectively, a large excess of heads or tails in a sequence of coin tosses) increases with the number of trials. By associating each of the $N$ coin tosses with a time step, (3) can be expressed as a function of the time $t$ as

Example (4)

$$\sigma = \sqrt{t}$$

This is the well-known '$t^{1/2}$law' of the standard deviation.

Although I have covered the normal distribution in the context of a particular example, it arises for a considerably greater variety of circumstances. If, instead of having only two possibilities for the result of a trial event, there is an entire range of possibilities, then for a large enough number of trials, the displacements $s$ would still follow the normal distribution. This is an example of the *Central Limit Theorem*, which is one of the most important results in the theory of probability. It also sometimes called the 'law of large numbers'. The validity of this statement relies crucially on the individual displacements being independent, ie, the probability of obtaining a particular result is not affected by preceding results.

What assumptions are needed to justify the use of the central limit theorem as a model for market behaviour? The answer is contained in the *Efficient Market Hypothesis*, which states that market prices are the result of a large number of investors who reach decisions independently based on the same (and, in fact, all available) information. Another underlying property that is postulated is that market prices are *Markovian*, which asserts that the present states of the market impounds all information contained the record of past prices. Thus, only the present value of a financial instrument is asserted to be relevant for predicting its future behaviour.

The important assumptions in the efficient market hypothesis are (i) the independence of the investors, (ii) the availability to all investors of all information, and (iii) the Markovian property of market prices. These assumptions are translated into the random walk model as, respectively, (i) independent coin tosses (or, more accurately, independent samplings of step lengths dictated by a certain distribution, as will be discussed in Section 4), (ii) the probabilities of possible outcomes of every coin toss being the same, and (iii) the outcome of any random event being independent of the results of preceding events. These properties, along with the Central Limit Theorem, which we can invoke because of the large number of investors, traders, etc., then imply that the distribution of prices should follow a normal distribution. It should also be mentioned, with reference to Section 2, that the efficient market hypothesis also asserts that markets are *linear* and that the randomness is of the simplest type.

A study of the distribution of returns was carried out in the late 1960s by Fama (1965), who compared five-day Standard & Poor returns from January 1928 and noted three differences compared with the normal distribution (Figure 2): the returns were slightly skewed in that there were more returns less than the mean than greater than the mean, the peak around the mean was considerably higher than in the normal distribution, and extreme values occurred more frequently than in the normal distribution, which assigns little likelihood to such values. More recent studies, which are compiled by Peters (1991a), have agreed with Fama's observations. Sterge (1989), in particular, studied financial futures prices of Treasury Bonds, Treasury Notes and Eurodollar contracts and also concluded that large deviations are vastly underestimated by the normal distribution. He writes that, '... very large (three or more standard deviations from the norm) price deviations can be expected to occur two to three times as often as predicted by normality'.

These studies bring into serious question the validity of

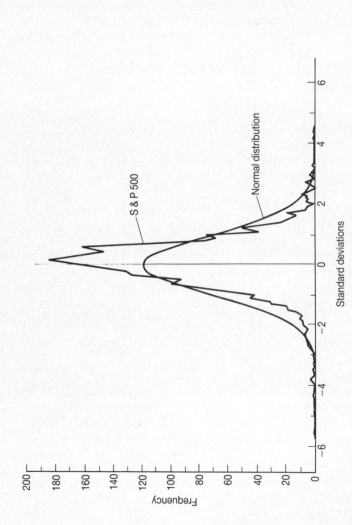

**Figure 2** Comparison of the frequency of Standard & Poor 500 five-day returns from January 1928–December 1989 with the normal distribution generated from the mean and standard deviation calculated from the frequencies (after *Peters* (1989)).

using normal distributions to describe markets which, in turn, raise doubts about the underlying assumptions of the efficient market hypothesis. Before considering possible resolutions of these discrepancies, I will examine some elaborations on the basic random walk model and its applications.

# 4. GENERALISED RANDOM WALKS

Although there are discrepancies between the normal distribution and the distribution of market returns, the random walk paradigm has nevertheless been generalised and applied with some success in a variety of special cases (see Varian (1992), for a review accompanied with computer packages). I summarise here several ways of how the simple random walk introduced in the preceding section can be generalised and then describe an application to the Black-Scholes model of option pricing.

The normal distribution in example 2 was seen to be characterised by two quantities, the mean and the rms deviation. For the coin toss model of the random walk the values were found to be $\mu = 0$ and $\sigma = b\sqrt{t}$. Suppose now that instead of the likelihood of heads and tails being equal, the probability of the coin landing heads is $p$ and the probability of it landing tails is $q$, and the related requirement that $p + q = 1$. It is then found that the mean and the standard deviation are given by

Example (5)

$$\mu = (p - q)t, \quad \sigma = 2\sqrt{pqt}$$

The average value of $s$ now increases (if $p > q$) or decreases (if $p < q$) proportionately to $t$ (the number of coin tosses). Because of this, the quantity $\mu$ is sometimes referred to as the *drift* of the process. The standard deviation still increases proportionately to $t\frac{1}{2}$ as in example 4, though with a different ratio. Figure 3 shows the behaviour of $s$ for a biased random walk for three sequences of 1000 steps. The values of $p$ and $q$ are chosen such that $p = 0.55$ and $q = 0.45$, *ie*, there is a 55 per cent chance that coin will land on heads and a 45 per cent chance that it will land on tails. Thus, according to equation (5), the drift of this process is $\mu = (0.55 - 0.45)$ $t = 0.1t$. This represents the average path taken and is shown in Figure 2 for comparison with each of the paths. The standard deviation for these values of $p$ and $q$ is given by $\sigma = 0.99\sqrt{t}$, which is close to that given in equation (4), so the spread in outcomes is expected to be approximately the same in Figures 1 and 2. Notice that the multiplicative factor is *smaller* than that for the case where $p = q = \frac{1}{2}$ because there is less uncertainty in the outcome.

By generalising this process even further by considering not a coin that gives only two possible results, but an event that samples from any number of possible results (whose probabilities add up to one), $\mu$ and $\sigma$ can still be calculated. The results of these calculations are expressed symbolically as

Example (6)

$$\mu = at, \quad a = b\sqrt{t}$$

for some numbers $a$ and $b$. A process like one we have just described, where a choice is made from any number (including an infinite number) of possible outcomes is called a *generalised Weiner process*. An example of such a process is a random walk for which the individual step lengths are chosen according to the Gaussian distribution in equation (2). This is called a *Gaussian random walk*. Steps of any length, positive or negative, can occur in a Gaussian random walk, but the probability of choosing a very long step diminishes rapidly with the length of the step.

A further generalisation of the random walk is also possible. If, in equation (6), we replace the *constants* $a$ and $b$ are replaced by *functions* of $s$ and $t$, then both the mean and the standard deviation depend on both $s$ and $t$ as well:

Example (7)

$$\mu = a(s,t)t, \quad s = b(s,t)\sqrt{t}$$

A process so characterised is called an *Ito process*. It might be easiest to think of an Ito process as being made up of

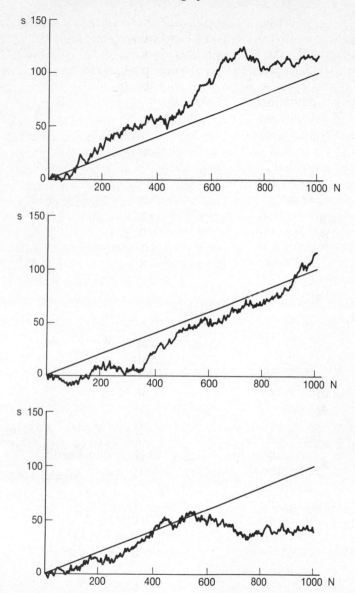

**Figure 3** The behaviour of a biased random walk during three sequences of 1000 steps. The solid line represents the average path and corresponds to the drift of the process. The values of *p* and *q* are chosen such that there is a 55 per cent chance that coin will land on heads and a 45 per cent chance that it will land on tails.

generalised Weiner processes whose means and variances depend on the instantaneous values of s and $t$. A review of the application of the Ito description to financial decision making has been given by Malliaris (1983). Merton (1975) argues that an Ito process is indeed a suitable approximation of the behaviour of certain economic variables.

The option pricing model of Black and Scholes (1973) provides an example where an Ito process has been used to obtain a tangible result (Hull 1993). Begin with an Ito process for a stock price, signified by $S$. Both the mean and the standard deviation of the stock must now be identified. The mean of the stock, or the drift, is determined by the expectation of investors that the increase of $S$ (*ie*, the instantaneous return) is some fraction of $S$ and that this fraction is independent of $S$. If this fraction is denoted by $r$:

Example (8)

$$\mu = rSt$$

It should be noted that if this was the only effect on the stock price, then the value of the stock at time $t$ would be

Example (9)

$$S(t) = S_0 e^{rt}$$

In this equation $S_0$ is the initial price of the stock. Equation (9) states that the price of the stock would grow at a continuously compounded rate of interest $r$ per unit of time.

It is now necessary to specify the standard deviation, or volatility, of the stock. The assumption that is made is that the uncertainty in the percentage return of the stock is the same regardless of the stock price. Thus, in analogy with equation (8):

Example (10)

$$\sigma = qS\sqrt{t}$$

where $q$ is the standard deviation of the proportional change in the stock price. Taken together, equations (8) and (10) state that the stock price follows an Ito process with the drift given by $rSt$ and the standard deviation by $qS\sqrt{t}$. The behaviour of the stock price implied by these choices of $\mu$ and $\sigma$ lead to what is called a *log normal* distribution for $S$, *ie*, the logarithm of $S$, rather than $S$ itself, follows a normal distribution (of equation (2)).

To obtain the equations of Black and Scholes (1973), suppose that $f$ is the price of a derivative security contingent upon the price $S$ of a particular stock. One consequence of this is that the underlying cause of the randomness of $f$ is the same as that for $S$. The basic idea of the Black-Scholes approach is that a suitably-chosen portfolio of the stock and the derivative security can eliminate the effect of the random process. The portfolio obtained is one that is *short* one derivative security and *long* on $\partial f / \partial S$ shares. The equation whose solution yields the function $f$ is called the *Black–Scholes differential equation*. A derivation may be found in the book by Hull (1993).

A huge literature has grown around the Black–Scholes model since its publication 20 years ago. A review of the assessment of this model and its many extensions has been given by Malliaris (1983). There are two points that should be noted immediately about the original Black–Scholes model. First, the solution $f$ of the Black–Scholes differential equation is a function of time. Thus, the portfolio must be changed continuously to maintain the risklessness. The second point relates to the assumptions regarding the interactions between derivatives and underlying markets, which are not generally known. The derivation used by Black–Scholes applied the methods developed by Ito, which provide a definite relationship between the randomness of the underlying asset and the derivative through what is known as *Ito's Theorem*. For more general types of randomness, this relationship may not be so constrained.

# 5. FRACTIONAL RANDOM WALKS – ARE MARKETS CHAOTIC?

The models described in the preceding sections rely on a Weiner process to generate the randomness, *ie*, the underlying randomness is the same as that generated by the flipping of a coin. In recent years an altogether different approach to studying erratic systems has emerged. Broadly speaking, this field has developed into what is known as 'chaos' (see Crutchfield *et al.* (1986) and Gleich (1987) for introductory discussions). The discovery has many important implications for the study and characterisation of many dynamical systems that exhibit eratic or apparently random behaviour. This behaviour is an intrinsic part of the equations; it is not due to any lack of information about the system. Thus, chaos provides limits to the predictability of these types of systems but also suggests that there may be an underlying pattern in what were previously regarded as randomly-generated data.

One of the earliest attempts to understand the behaviour of complex systems in terms of simple dynamical systems was the work carried out by Edward Lorenz in the early 1960s. Lorenz attempted to understand the unpredictability of the weather by simplifying the basic equations of fluid flow to the point where only three quantities varied with time. Despite this simplicity, the solution of these equations behaved in an apparently random fashion. To analyse the origin of this behaviour, Lorenz used a digital computer and found that the cause for the randomness is the amplification of small differences to macroscopic proportions. Thus, if two points are allowed to travel along nearby solutions of the equations, the paths of these points first diverge very quickly, but are then drawn together, then diverge again and so on. The resulting picture that emerges is one similar to shuffling a pack of cards, where two cards initially adjacent to one another are separated, but are again adjacent at some later time, whereupon the act of shuffling separates them again.

The question naturally arises as to whether the market returns exhibit such behaviour. One of the most powerful features of the theory of chaos is the ability to analyse time series, *ie*, records in time of a quantity such as daily market returns or the daily highs and lows of temperatures in a region. I will focus on one such method developed by Hurst initially for the analysis of water levels in reservoirs (Hurst *et al.* (1965), Feder, (1988)).

To appreciate the analysis used by Hurst, and its applicability to a wide range of time series, including market returns, I will describe briefly the problem Hurst was trying to solve, namely, the design of an ideal reservoir with an adjacent lake. An ideal reservoir neither overflows nor empties. In a given year, $t$, the reservoir will accept an amount of water $w(t)$ from the lake and a regulated volume will be released from the reservoir. The problem is to determine the storage required for the reservoir to release an amount of water each year equal to the average influx for the period under consideration. The average arithmetic influx $<w>$ over $N$ years is calculated in the usual way as

Example (11)

$$<w> = \frac{1}{N} [w(1) + w(2) + \cdots + w(N)]$$

This average should be equal to the volume released per year from the reservoir. Let $X(t)$ denote the accumulated departure from the average $<w>$ of the influx $w(t)$:

Example (12)

$$X(t) = \sum_{i=1}^{N} [w(t) - <w>]$$

The difference between the maximum and minimum values attained by $X$ is called the range and is denoted $R(t)$. The range is the storage capacity of the reservoir required to maintain the average discharge of water throughout the period considered and represents the difference between the maximum and minimum amounts of water contained in the reservoir. The range is also a function of time, since it is expected to increase as the time span increases.

Hurst investigated many time series for different types of phenomena. To compare the observed ranges of different quantities, Hurst divided the range $R(t)$ by the standard deviation of the entire time series (cf. equation (3)), which Hurst denoted by $S$. The quantity $R/S$ is dimensionless, *ie*, it is a pure number, and so can be compared across many types of phenomena that are measured by different quantities, such as river discharges, temperatures, pressures, and sunspot numbers. Hurst found that for many time series, $R/S$ is well described by the simple relation

Example (13)

$$R/S = (t/2)^H$$

The exponent $H$ (which was called $K$ by Hurst) is now known as the *Hurst exponent*. Hurst found that the value of $H$ for many time series generated by natural phenomena was near 0.7.

To interpret the meaning of the Hurst exponent, consider a generalisation of the random walk introduced in Section 3. This generalisation includes memory effects, *ie*, past results are correlated with future results, and are known as *fractional random walks* (Mandelbrot and Van Ness 1968, Mandelbrot 1982, Feder 1988). The effect of the memory in fractional random walks can be 'tuned' to produce any Hurst exponent in the range $0 \leqslant H \leqslant 1$. There are three ranges that characterise different types of behaviour for time series: (i) $0.5 \leqslant H \leqslant 1$ – a Hurst exponent in this range characterises a time series with persistent or trend-reinforcing behaviour (see figure 4). An increasing trend in the past implies an increasing trend in the future (on average) and, similarly, a decreasing trend in the past implies (on average) a decreasing trend in the future; (ii) $H = 0.5$: – there is no correlation between past and future events, *ie*, there is no memory in the events recorded by the time series. An example of such a process is the random walk discussed in Section 3; (iii) $0 \leqslant H \leqslant 0.5$ – a time series with a Hurst exponent in this range shows anti-persistent or trend-reversing behaviour. An increasing trend in the past implies a *decreasing* trend in the future (on average) and, similarly a decreasing trend in the past implies (on average) an *increasing* trend in the future. Technical details of fractional Brownian motion and related topics may be found in the book by Feder (1988), and in the series of articles by Mandelbrot and Wallis (1969a–c).

For time series of natural phenomena, a positive Hurst exponent implies that there are correlations in the phenomena being measured, with the value near 0.7 indicating trend-

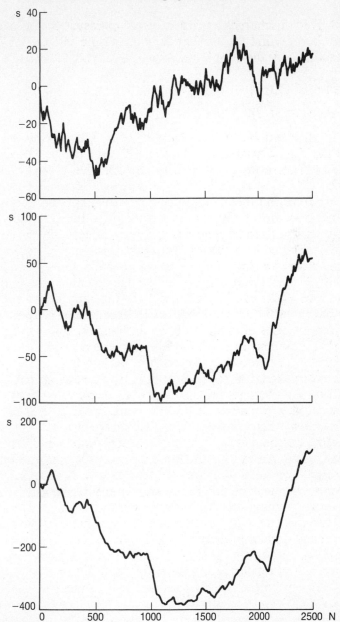

**Figure 4** Fractional random walks for three sequences of 1000 steps with Hurst exponents of 0.5 (top), 0.7 (centre) and 0.9 (bottom). Notice that as the Hurst exponent increases, the deviations of the random walk also increase and the small-scale noise decreases (after *Feder* 1988).

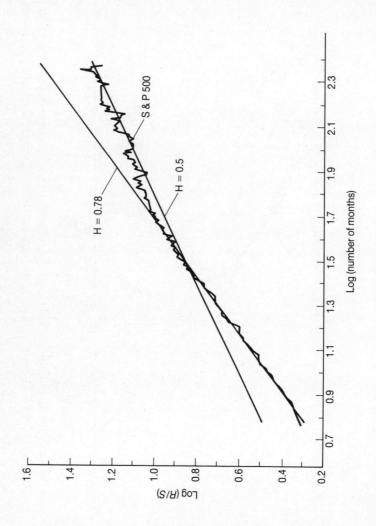

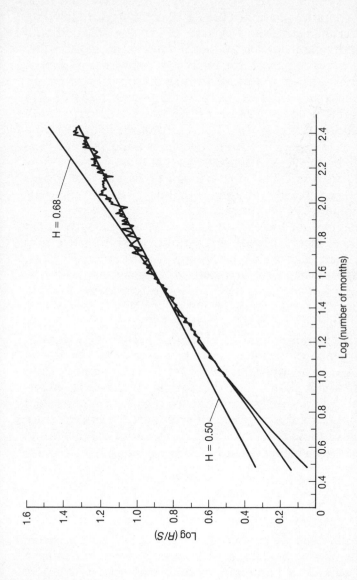

**Figure 5** *R/S* analysis of Standard & Poor 500 monthly returns from January 1950–July 1988 (top) and for 30-year Treasury Bond yields taken monthly from January 1950–December 1989 (bottom) (after *Peters* (1989)).

reinforcing behaviour. Do financial markets exhibit such behaviour as well? Peters (1989, 1991b) has analysed a wide variety of markets using Hurst's $R/S$ analysis, including currency exchange rates, Treasury Bill yields, international stocks, individual stocks and Standard & Poor monthly returns. Two examples of this analysis are shown in Figure 5. Peters observed two important features in these diagrams. In almost every case, the Hurst exponent is greater than 0.5, with most markets producing $H$ near 0.7, though a few have both higher and lower values. In addition, for large enough times, the value of $H$ crosses over to 0.5, which is indicative of a time series with no memory. This suggests that these markets show persistent behaviour for short enough times but over longer times are completely random. For the Standard & Poor returns, this time is 48 months.

The results shown in Figure 3 are very thought-provoking. Because the time series of these returns exhibit effects of memory, these markets do not follow a random walk. Thus, the behaviour of these markets is inconsistent with the efficient market hypothesis. On a more fundamental, these results suggest (but certainly do not prove) that these markets might be chaotic dynamical systems. In terms of the points made earlier in this section, the repeated periods of adjacency and divergence of chaotic systems may be the underlying cause of the behaviour seen in Figure 5. The comparison in Figure 2, which shows that the normal distribution under-estimates large deviation from the average is also consistent with the trend-reinforcing behaviour implied by Figure 3. An exposition of these ideas and their implications may be found in the book by Peters (1991a).

# 6. SUMMARY

A survey has been given of methods that are currently used in the mathematical modelling of market movements using a random walk as a paradigm of different types of random processes. Although applications of many of these methods can claim individual triumphs, there does not appear to be framework within which to analyse market behaviour that is based on a well-founded set of assumptions. This, in part, is due to the limited availability of data, but also to the complex nature of the system. Foremost among the sources of this complexity is the nature and characterisation of the random behaviour of markets. It is in this arena that methods of data analysis developed for studying simple chaotic systems have shown some striking results. Nevertheless, this approach only provides a characterisation of the data and does not necessarily yield a mathematical model. Thus, while the analysis described in Section 5 can put bounds on the predictability of market prices, without the underlying equations that generated the data, the harnessing of this information is severely hampered.

# References

Black, F. and Scholes, M. (1973). 'The Pricing of Options and Corporate Liabilities', *Journal of Political Economy* 81, pp. 637–59.

Crutchfield, J.P., Farmer, J.D., Packard, N.H. and Shaw, R.S. (1986). 'Chaos', *Scientific American* 255(7), pp. 38–49.

Drazin, P.G. and King, G.P., eds. *Interpretation of Time Series for Nonlinear Systems* (Amsterdam: North Holland, 1992), *Physica D* 58.

Fama, E.F. (1965). 'The Behaviour of Stock Market Prices', *Journal of Business* 38, pp. 34–105.

Feder, J., *Fractals* (New York, Plenum 1988).

Gleick, J., *Chaos: Making a New Science* (New York: Viking Press, 1987).

Hull, J.C. (1993). *Options, Futures, and other Derivative Securities* 2nd edition (Englewood Cliffs, NJ, Prentice Hall).

Hurst, H.E., Black, R.P. and Simaika, Y.M. (1965). *Long-Term Storage: An Experimental Study* (London, Constable).

Larrain, M., 'Testing Chaos and Nonlinearities in T-Bill Rates', *Financial Analysts Journal* 47(5) (1991), pp. 51–62.

Malliaris, A.G. (1983). 'Ito's Calculus in Financial Decision Making', *Society for Industrial and Applied Mathematics Review* 25, pp. 481–496.

Mandelbrot, B.B. (1982). *The Fractal Geometry of Nature* (New York, W.H. Freeman).

Mandelbrot, B.B. and Van Ness, J.W. (1968). 'Fractional Brownian

Motion, Fractional Noises and Applications', *Society of Industrial and Applied Mathematics Review* 10, pp. 422–437.

Mandelbrot, B.B. and Wallis, J.R., 'Computer Experiments with Fractional Gaussian Noises. Part 1, Averages and Variances', *Water Resources Research* 5 (1969a), pp. 228–241.

Mandelbrot B.B., and Wallis, J.R., 'Computer Experiments with Fractional Gaussian Noises. Part 2, Rescaled Ranges and Spectra', *Water Resources Research* 5 (1969b), pp. 242–259.

Mandelbrot B.B. and Wallis, J.R., 'Computer Experiments with Fractional Gaussian Noises. Part 3, Mathematical Appendix', *Water Resources Research* 5 (1969c), pp. 260–267.

Merton, R.C. (1975), 'Theory of Finance from the Perspective of Continuous Time', *Journal of Financial and Quantitative Analysis* 10, pp. 659–674.

Peters, E.A. (1989), 'Fractal Structure in the Capital Markets', *Financial Analysts Journal*,45(4), pp. 32–37.

Peters, E.A. (1991a). *Chaos and Order in the Capital Markets* (New York, Wiley).

Peters, E.A. (1991b). 'R/S Analysis using Logarithmic Returns: A Technical Note', *Financial Analysts Journal*, 47.

Sterge, A.J. (1989). 'On the Distribution of Financial Futures Price Changes', *Financial Analysts Journal*, 45(3) pp. 75–78.

Varian, H.R., ed., *Economic and Financial Modeling with Mathematica* (New York: Springer, 1992).

## Chapter 9

# PRINCIPLES OF NETTING IN FINANCIAL AND COMMODITIES MARKETS[1]

## Philip Wood,
## Allen & Overy

## 1. BACKGROUND

The purpose of this chapter is to review the role of netting for the safety and efficiency of markets and to identify the legal principles governing the legal efficacy of netting.

In the interests of clarity, this chapter simplifies the issues by way of orientation and is not legal advice. Comments on the laws of jurisdictions other than England should be treated cautiously.

At its simplest, netting is the ability to set off reciprocal claims on the insolvency of a counterparty. If party A owes party B £100 million and party B owes party A £100 million and if party B becomes insolvent, then if party A can set-off, his exposure is zero. If he cannot, his exposure is £100 million.

Over recent decades there has been an explosion in the size of markets. Apart from the traditional markets for the sale of commodities (such as produce, metals and oil) and the securities markets, these markets include the money and foreign exchange markets, payment systems, and newer markets involving futures, options, interest swaps and the like.

The daily volume in these markets is colossal, especially in the world's financial centres. The result is a potentially huge exposure of market participants, and those who finance those participants, to the failure of a major participant with consequent risk of cascading insolvencies – the domino or

1. © P. Wood, 1993

systemic risk. There may be pressures on the public purse to rescue the situation so that the risk could be passed back to the taxpayer.

The objects of netting are: to reduce those exposures and hence to protect the integrity of financial institutions and the financial system. (The reduction in risk can be dramatic, *eg* more than 90 per cent. The reduction in exposure is reflected in reduced capital adequacy costs and an improved balance sheet); to reduce transaction costs, such as the cost of maintaining credit lines and margin to cover gross exposures, and to reduce the cost of processing a multiplicity of gross contracts.

Since the exposures are so large, a high degree of legal predictability is required – the same degree of certainty one would expect of a mortgage.

Netting is primarily (but not exclusively) a matter of insolvency law, not the governing law of the contract concerned. The contract must, of course, be valid outside insolvency law, but generally this does not present significant legal problems in the ordinary case beyond the usual precautions applicable to all contracts.

Netting is often merely another term for set-off. But the term 'netting' is used by the markets because in many cases the process involves more than just a set-off of debts.

There are two main categories of netting – settlement netting and default netting – and these may now be examined.


## 2. SETTLEMENT NETTING

Settlement netting is intended to reduce settlement risks, *ie* the risk that one party pays or delivers and the other becomes bankrupt before he pays or delivers. The risk arises because it is often impracticable to arrange simultaneous payment and delivery.

This type of netting is variously called 'settlement netting' or 'delivery netting' or 'payments netting'.

For example, if bank A is to pay yen to bank B under a foreign exchange contract in return for US dollars, then bank

A may be obliged to pay the yen through the Tokyo clearing system before New York opening when the US dollars can be paid by bank B. If bank B becomes insolvent after receiving the yen but before paying the dollars, bank A has a gross exposure.

If, however, in the above example bank A and bank B had a series of US dollar/yen and yen/US dollar contracts between themselves for the same value date and agreed to net out the deliveries as soon as the contracts with a common currency arose, then the delivery exposures could be greatly reduced (see Figure 1).

Settlement netting is therefore a contract to net, in advance of the settlement date, reciprocal obligations for the same class of asset for the same settlement date. The netting can equally be applied to payments, foreign exchange deliveries, commodities and securities.

Settlement netting raises relatively few legal issues when compared to default netting and is straightforward from the documentary point of view.

One of the main legal issues concerns preferences, *ie* insolvency doctrines providing for the disgorge of a transfer which the debtor makes in favour of a creditor in the suspect period prior to the opening of the formal insolvency proceedings and which prejudice other creditors of the debtor. The main object of these rules is to prevent transfers by a debtor who is actually insolvent which prefer the transferee ahead of other creditors. The agreed early discharge or 'payment' of reciprocal obligations must not be a preference voidable on insolvency.

The essence of a preference is improvement in the position of the creditor, *ie* the result of the transaction is that the creditor's position is better on the insolvency of the counterparty than it would have been if the transaction had not occurred. The transaction must usually have taken place in the suspect period (varying in the different countries from three months to eighteen months) and at a time when the counterparty is actually insolvent.

It will generally be found that, if the contracts concerned would be eligible for the second type of netting discussed below (default netting), settlement netting does not improve

**Figure 1 Settlement Risk**

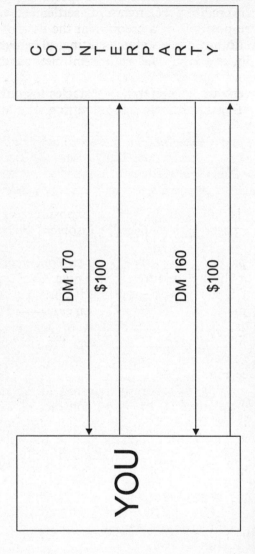

COUNTERPARTY

DM 170

$100

DM 160

$100

YOU

Gross settlement exposure to counterparty:
DM170 + $100
Net exposure: DM10

*Source:* Allen & Overy

the position of the creditor. This is because the position of the insolvent on a close-out is the same, whether or not settlement netting had taken place: there is no prejudice to the insolvent's other creditors. Conversely, settlement netting does improve the position of a creditor in the case of those countries which do not allow default netting, although even here it is usually the case that settlement netting can be protected.

In England there are no preference obstacles to settlement netting (because England allows default netting, and also for other reasons).

## 3. DEFAULT NETTING

Default netting is intended to reduce exposures on open contracts if one party should become insolvent before the settlement date.

For example, party A and party B have two open contracts between them for the sale of foreign exchange. One contract shows a profit of 5, the other a loss of 5. If party B becomes insolvent before maturity and if party A can cancel and set off losses and gains, party A's exposure to his insolvent counterparty would be zero. If, however, the cancellation and set-off were not possible, party A would have a gross exposure of 5 (see Figure 2).

This type of netting is variously referred to as 'default netting' or 'close-out netting' or 'open contract netting' or 'replacement contract netting' – the precise vernacular or colloquialism does not matter. The essence of the netting is that the innocent party revokes all his unperformed contracts with the insolvent and sets off gains and losses on those contracts.

From the technical point of view, the legal conditions for the efficacy of this type of netting depend upon the class of contract. Although there are a number of variants, most market contracts fall into one of the following two categories:

(a) The first is a contract involving the payment of a vested debt or unliquidated claim. Here, it must simply

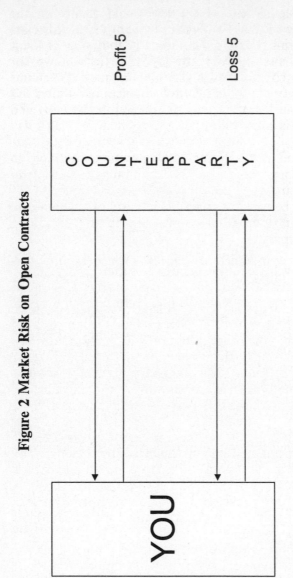

**Figure 2 Market Risk on Open Contracts**

Gross market exposure to counterparty: 5
Net market exposure to counterparty: zero

*Source:* Allen & Overy

be possible to set off the reciprocal claims on the insolvency of the counterparty. Examples of this class are (i) claims for simple liquidated debts, such as loans and deposits already made, and (ii) claims for unliquidated or contingent debts, such as claims under contracts for differences (typical of futures and options markets) and claims under interest caps and floors. This is something of a simplification, but it will suffice.

(b) The second category includes executory contracts to deliver property or money. Here, it must be possible to do two things:

it must be possible to rescind, cancel or terminate all open or unmatured contracts with the defaulting counterparty;

it must be possible to set off resulting losses and gains over the whole series of mutual contracts.

Examples of the second type of contract include (i) contracts for the sale of commodities, bullion, securities or other property, and (ii) contracts for the exchange or delivery of money, such as normal foreign exchange contracts, interest swaps, and obligations to place a deposit. English case law has established that foreign exchange contracts fall into this category in the sense that each party's claim against the other is for damages if the other does not perform – usually the extra cost of buying the defaulted currency in the market. They are not reciprocal debts. In other words, the remedies under a foreign exchange contract are the same as the remedies under a contract of barter of goods, *eg* exchanging peas and beans. It is thought that normal interest swaps would fall into the same category. This characterisation entirely accords with the practices of the markets concerned.

The difference is exemplified by the remedy of a depositor against a bank for non-payment of a deposit of 100 (debt claim for 100) and the remedy of a borrower against a lender for failure by the lender to make a loan of 100 (extra cost to the borrower of getting the loan elsewhere, *eg* five, but not 100).

Although both are claims for money in the amount of 100, the remedies and the amounts payable on a default are very different since the contracts are different in nature.

If the solvent counterparty is not able to rescind all the open contracts and to set off, then the insolvency administrator of the other party may be able to 'cherry-pick', *ie* claim selective performance of the profitable contracts and repudiate the unprofitable contracts. The result would be that it would not be possible to net out the loss and gain of five and five.

In one group of countries, cherry-picking is seen as fair: they say that the insolvency administrator ought to be able to claim profits so that he can enlarge the estate available to unsecured creditors, or at least to employees as preferential creditors. But in another group of countries, it is seen as unjust that the insolvent defaulter should be able to insist on payment of profits, but nevertheless refuse to pay losses – dividends payable by insolvent estates are rarely more than 10 per cent. Contrary to the view in debtor-orientated countries, their policy is to help creditors to escape the debacle. They support this policy by the view that it is unreasonable that a defaulter should be paid, but not pay.

Whatever view is taken about the philosophic morality of the matter or the public interest, the absence of international legal harmony poses risks for market participants and a perceptible degree of legal risk (in addition to credit risks) which has to be specifically evaluated.

# 4. DEFAULT NETTING IN ENGLAND

English insolvency law allows default netting as against ordinary banks and corporates.

As mentioned, in the case of one class of transaction, both rescission and set-off must be available and in the other class only set-off is necessary.

As to rescission, there is no objection to the cancellation of an executory contract for the sale of unidentified assets under an express rescission clause operating on default, including insolvency. If a seller agrees to sell grain not yet identified for delivery in three months and the buyer becomes bankrupt after one month, the seller can cancel the contract if the contract allows him to do so. The same principle applies to foreign exchange contracts.

English insolvency law does not nullify these rescission clauses. Case law supports this conclusion and indeed close-outs under the rules of stock exchange and commodity markets have given rise to a long series of cases going back to the nineteenth century, none of which challenged the efficacy of the close-out. A claim under an executory contract of this type by the insolvent is not treated as an asset of the estate which cannot be removed on insolvency.

The result is paralleled by the law on the cancellation of other contracts on insolvency, such as licences, equipment leases, obligations to make a loan and the like.

If there is no express rescission clause, netting is still possible, but the solvent['s] party's position is different. The debtor's insolvency will often amount to an implied repudiation entitling the counterparty to cancel in any event. If in the circumstances there is no implied repudiation (*eg* because the insolvency administrator immediately gives adequate assurances of performance), it would normally still not be possible for the insolvency administrator to compel the creditor to perform by an action for specific performance since specific performance is not generally available for contracts for unascertained assets readily available elsewhere in the market. The innocent party would at the most be obliged to pay damages (if the insolvency administrator is ready and willing to perform), but these damages would be eligible for set-off against losses payable by the defaulter on other repudiated contracts.

The result would merely at worst reflect the common market practice of two-way payments, *ie* each side accounts to the other for profits. Two-way payments are discussed in section 8 below.

As to set-off, the English policy in favour of insolvency set-off in the Insolvency Rules 1986 r.4.90 is so strong that the set-off is mandatory. Insolvency set-off has been statutory since 1705 and has been the subject of a vast body of highly predictable and well settled case law. In the case of the first class of obligation (vested non-executory claims), the claims are set-off. In the case of the second class of contract, all losses and gains arising from pre-petition cancelled contracts between the parties would be brought into account and a net balance would be payable either way. This set-off operates to net losses and gains of executory contracts entered into prior to the insolvency order and also to set-off ordinary debts, even though the contracts are closed-out or the debts mature after the insolvency date. The claims do not have to be connected or arise out of the same or related transactions or under the same master agreement.

Rescission of executory contracts and set-off are not affected by an administration order or voluntary arrangement under the Insolvency Act 1986. Both are, broadly, corporate rehabilitation procedures as an alternative to final liquidation. Administrations stay creditor proceedings and steps to enforce security or to repossess, but not self-help contract rescissions of this type or set-off. However, in the case of a voluntary arrangement, there should be an appropriate event of default allowing a close-out before the creditors meeting to approve the proposal for a voluntary arrangement. The event should crystallise on notice of the creditor's meeting being given. This is to avoid the counterparty being bound by a creditor resolution effectively staying the close-out (see Figure 3).

# 5. DEFAULT NETTING: INTERNATIONAL COMPARISON

International comparisons reveal a great diversity of approach to the rescission of executory contracts and set-off on insolvency.

Broadly speaking, one group of states (which includes England) allows creditors to protect themselves against a potential defaulter, *eg* by rescinding contracts and by set-off; while another group seeks to preserve assets of the debtor's

Figure 3 Set-off and Corporate Rehabilitation

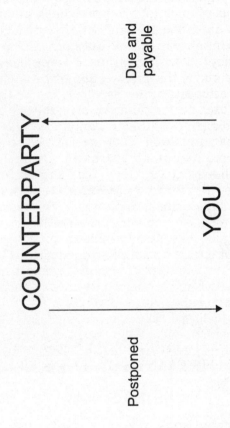

estate with a view to the rehabilitation or protection of the debtor, *eg* by preventing the rescission of profitable contracts and by limiting insolvency set-off.

One of the policies underlying both rescission and set-off is that it is seen as inequitable that the insolvent should be able to insist on performance when he himself refuses to perform.

Prohibitions on rescission and set-off are more likely to arise in the case of rehabilitation proceedings intended to encourage the survival of the debtor. Netting must survive the rehabilitation statute, as well as final liquidation.

As to rescission of executory contracts, most developed bankruptcy laws give the insolvency administrator the right to accept or reject contracts of the insolvent, so that the main question is whether the administrator, in calling for performance of profitable contracts, can ignore a cancellation clause in the contract itself. There seem to be only a few states which expressly nullify rescission clauses. These jurisdictions include France, New Zealand (under the optional statutory management procedure which can only be initiated by the government and which is extraordinary) and the United States. But the United States automatic stay on rescission clauses has been removed under complex statutory exceptions in order to allow netting, but only in the case of certain counterparties and certain contracts. Careful attention must be paid to the detailed conditions on which the reliefs are predicated.

Conversely, it is believed that countries such as Germany, Austria, Japan, Belgium, Italy, Switzerland and many others (as well as numerous states basing their insolvency law on the English model) do not nullify rescission clauses in executory contracts of this type.

As to set-off, a bloc of jurisdictions forbids insolvency set-off altogether, subject to limited exceptions. These include France, Luxembourg, Spain, Greece and their related jurisdictions. Insolvency set-off is seen as contravening the *pari passu* principle and hence the creditor must pay in what he owes and prove for what he is owed. But even in these countries, it is commonly the case that insolvency set-off is available if the cross-claims are connected or if they arise in the same current account.

On the other hand, insolvency set-off of mutual claims is specifically permitted by statute in perhaps the majority of the leading jurisdictions including England, Germany, Japan, Austria, Switzerland, Italy, Norway, Denmark, Finland, Scotland (non-statutory), Sweden, the Netherlands, and, again, the numerous jurisdictions basing their insolvency law on English bankruptcy legislation, such as Australia, Hong Kong and Singapore. Recent insolvency legislation in Australia has not affected set-off (or contract rescission).

The contrast is shown by the fact that in England insolvency set-off is not merely permitted, but is mandatory and the parties cannot contract out, whereas in France insolvency set-off is prohibited and one cannot contract in.

# 6. CONTRACTUAL ENHANCEMENTS

Markets responded to the potential bars on rescission and set-off in the hostile jurisdictions by two contractual devices:

(1) The first is a provision that all contracts between the parties are automatically deemed to be cancelled and losses and gains set off immediately prior to the institution of insolvency proceedings. The hope is that a cancellation and a set-off automatically deemed to take place immediately prior to the insolvency would not be subject to the nullification of rescission clauses and the bar on insolvency set-off which come into effect on the opening of the insolvency proceedings – they have already occurred. This is the origin of the automatic termination clause.

(2) The second device is to seek to take advantage of the common exemption from the bar on rescission and set-off (in countries hostile to netting) which exists in favour of contracted transactions. For example, an insolvent cannot claim the price for goods sold without allowing a deduction for defects in the goods – the classic connexity situation which is recognised everywhere. A master contract entered into between the parties provides that all of the individual trades between the parties are governed by the umbrella master agreement and all those trades are connected transactions as

part of the same business relationship. The theory is that, although the insolvency administrator may be able to cherry-pick by selective performance of individual contracts and repudiation of the rest, he could not do so in the case of a single transaction, *ie* he could not claim to take the benefit of one part of the transaction without also assuming its burden if it is all one bargain. He should not be able to take the cream without the crust, the cherry without the pip, the rose without the thorn. Plainly connexity between different contracts for different value dates and for different products is more remote than in the case of a single transaction. The contractual connexity is sometimes reinforced by a provision that all new contracts between the parties are novated so as to form a single contract with existing contracts. These contractual provisions are the origin of connexity by master contracts and of netting by novation.

The key question is whether a private contract – whether automatic termination on contractual connexity or novation – can defeat a bankruptcy statue which expressly nullifies set-off or rescission or both. This is a matter for local law. If the contracting-out defies a statutory prohibition, it must be capable of strong and convincing legal justification if the requirement of predictability is to be satisfied.

Automatic cancellation, connexity and novation are not necessary for the validity of default netting under English law.

## 7. STATUTORY ENHANCEMENT OF INSOLVENCY NETTING

Such is the priority accorded to the legal validity of market netting, that at least nine states have enacted special provisions of varying scope which enhance netting on insolvency. The jurisdictions include:

| | |
|---|---|
| *Austria* | s.22 of the Bankruptcy Act (mandatory rescission of certain market contracts) |
| *Belgium* | Article 157 of Law of 19 April 1993 (netting between credit institutions) |

| | |
|---|---|
| *Canada* | s.65.1(7) to (9) of the Bankruptcy Act, inserted in 1992, applying to certain financial contracts |
| *England* | Part VII of the Companies Act 1989 (applying mainly to certain recognised organisations and largely declaratory of existing netting law) |
| *Germany* | s.18 of the Bankruptcy Act of 1879 (mandatory rescission of certain market contracts) |
| *Italy* | Article 76 of the Bankruptcy Act (mandatory rescission of certain market contracts) |
| *Japan* | Article 61 of the Bankruptcy Law (applying to exchange quoted merchandise) |
| *Netherlands* | s.38 of the Bankruptcy Act (mandatory rescission of certain market contracts) |
| *United States* | ss. 555 and 556 of the Bankruptcy Code of 1978 (applying to certain market contracts); s.212 of the Financial Institutions Reform, Recovery and Enforcement Act of 1989 (applying to certain contracts of federally insured banks and savings institutions); 1990 amendments to Bankruptcy Code (applying to swaps); 1991 Improvement Act. |

The provisions in Germany, Austria, the Netherlands, Japan and Italy are all similar. These provisions seem to have been based on the notion that in volatile markets an insolvent party should not have to wait to see if the administrator wishes to perform, particularly if it was unlikely that the defaulter would be able to perform. the netting clauses applied only to contracts in commodities markets and not expressly to financial contracts: this is because the sections are of respectable antiquity (1879 in Germany) when financial markets had not surmounted commodities markets in terms of size. To that extent they are quite limited. But in certain cases the provisions have been extended by case law to contracts for the sale of securities and in Italy the provisions have been extended to foreign exchange contracts by case law. The other jurisdictions might take the same view. In any event, it is believed to be the case that, in these five countries, it is not necessary that the contract comes within the special netting clause since the insolvency laws do not nullify express rescission clauses and set-off is statutorily permitted on a general basis – at least in the case of bankruptcy proceedings. The position in relation to the various Italian rehabilitation proceedings is complex.

The netting statutes in Belgium, Canada and the United States only apply to the specific contracts between the specific institutions specified in the legislation. Legislation was necessary in those jurisdictions, because the insolvency statute specifically prohibited rescission clauses or set-off or both. The US Bankruptcy Code of 1978, for example, is generally regarded as debtor-protective and froze most rescission clauses under the automatic stay provision. It was this stay which originally led to the development of the contractual devices reviewed in section.

England, by contrast, has had statutes mandating insolvency set-off continuously for nearly 300 years and it has not been necessary to deal with rescission clauses since that is the law in any event. The 1989 legislation in favour of certain recognised institutions and exchanges was largely declaratory so far as netting is concerned.

# 8. TWO-WAY PAYMENTS AND WALK-AWAY CLAUSES

If a bankrupt defaults on an executory contract, then he is liable to the creditor for damages – normally the extra cost to the creditor of obtaining the asset elsewhere in the market, compared to the contract price. If on the other had the contract is profitable to the defaulter, but the creditor cancels, then the creditor can himself sell the asset in the market at a profit.

If the creditor agrees to account to the defaulting insolvent for the profit, then the default payments are two-way – the insolvent pays losses and receives profits. If the creditor can keep profits, then he effectively walks away.

Many organised markets operate on the basis of full two-way payments and indeed the rules of the traditional London metals, commodities and stock markets have so provided since the early years of this century, if not before.

As a matter of law, full two-way payments are not necessary for the validity of the netting of executory contracts under English law, even though the effect of walk-away clauses is to deprive the insolvent estate of an asset in the form of the profit on the contract. This is not a penalty under English law, nor is it regarded as a void attempt to snatch away an asset of the insolvent which should be available to his creditors. Indeed, the cases on close-outs in the commodities markets reveal a judicial antipathy to two-way clauses whereby the insolvent is entitled to gains on his default – the clause must be clear if the defaulter is to have a benefit. But the cancellation of a vested asset of the insolvent (such as a deposit or (probably) a claim under a contract for differences), as opposed to the profit under an executory contract, would offend insolvency law. This is not a flaw, because these claims are eligible for set-off and cancellation is not required.

The position in other jurisdictions varies. Under certain of the statutory regimes mentioned above, full two-way payments are compulsory in the case of the contracts to which the legislation applies, *eg* in Germany. Many practitioners regard it as prudent to provide for full two-way payments in order to meet potential insolvency objections to asset-deprivation in jurisdictions which do not necessarily adopt the English view of two-way payments.

## 9. INTERVENERS

The safety of the netting of losses and gains on open contracts would be threatened if an intervener, who takes over the benefit of the counterparty's contract, could claim the contract free of netting against other contracts. The main interveners are attaching creditors (whether prejudgment or post-judgment), assignees and chargees of the counterparty, and undisclosed principals of the counterparty. An example is where a judgment creditor of the counterparty attaches claims owing to the counterparty, or some of them. The question is whether the innocent party may cancel contracts, the benefit of which the intervener has taken over, and set off losses on other contracts owing by the original counterparty so as to reduce the claim taken over by the intervener (see Figure 4).

There seems invariably to be no objection to cancelling contracts taken over by an intervener, but there should be an appropriate event of default. Hence the only question is whether the innocent party can set off against the intervener.

These interveners do not present a problem in England in a properly drafted netting agreement because the general position is that the intervener will take subject to the close-out and set-off if, before the innocent party has notice of the intervener, (a) the contract to set-off has been entered into and (b) both of the contracts given rise to the reciprocal claims have been entered into. In other words, a subsequent intervener cannot upset a contractual set-off which would have been exercisable if he had not intervened. The unnotified intervener loses priority to a close-out which has already been contractually set up, even though the close-out is exercised after the intervention.

In a number of jurisdictions, however, the set-off must be exercisable prior to notice of the intervener, *ie* the cancellation of contracts so as to mature the claims must take place before that time. This is often impracticable, *eg* the innocent party cannot be sure of being able to rescind prior to receiving notice of an attaching creditor. This adverse rule prevails in France and related jurisdictions. However, the law in some of these countries may protect transactionally-related claims – connexity on the grounds that the intervener cannot take the benefit of part of a transaction without being subject to the burdens.

Choice of law and exclusive jurisdiction clauses in favour of a favourable jurisdiction can be considered if there is a potential intervener problem.

Interveners have often not been viewed as a major impediment. This may be because experience has shown that the attachment of market contracts is unusual.

Figure 4 Set-off and Intervener Risk

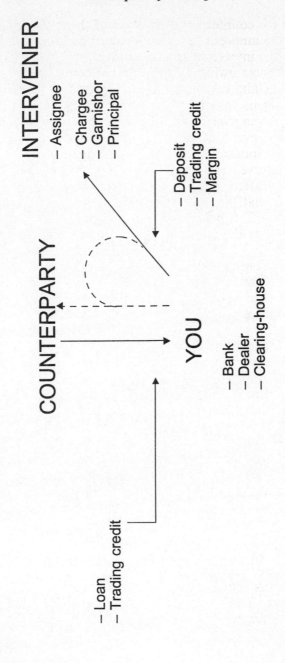

*Source:* Allen & Overy

## 10. MUTUALITY

The law obviously cannot permit a counterparty faced with a
liability to use somebody else's debt to set-off against that
liability: the counterparty would be expropriating a third
party's property to pay the counterparty's debt. Hence, the
doctrine of mutuality.

For insolvency set-off to operate, it is everywhere the rule
that the reciprocal claims must be mutual. This means that
there must be only two debtor-creditors: each must be
personally liable on the claim he owes to the other and each
must be solely and beneficially entitled to the claim he is owed
by the other, *ie* each is liable on one, owner of the other.
Mutuality does not mean that the debts have to be connected
or in the same currency or of the same type.

Typical examples of non-mutual debts are claims owed by
and to parent and subsidiary.

A common application of the rule arises where a party is
acting as agent.

It appears universally true that netting is not possible in
broker markets where counterparties act as agents on behalf
of their clients, notably in securities markets if the obligations
owed by a counterparty to the agent are held by that agent as
fiduciary or for the benefit of his outside client and do not
belong beneficially to himself. Any set-off against that claim
would not be possible because it results in the principal's
claim being used to pay the agent's personal liability, contrary
to the principle of mutuality (see Figure 5).

It is immaterial that, as is commonly the case, market
agents have personal liability to each other since mutuality
requires, not only reciprocal personal liability, but also that
each party owns the claims owed to it by the other beneficially
for itself and not on behalf of outside clients.

Dealing with this risk might require institutional changes in
traditional agency markets with consequent redistribution of
risks. It would require the removal of agency in favour of
principal relationships and hence (among other things) an
increased exposure of outside lay clients to their brokers.

Netting contracts should prohibit the parties from

**Figure 5 Multiple clients (presence of clients known)**

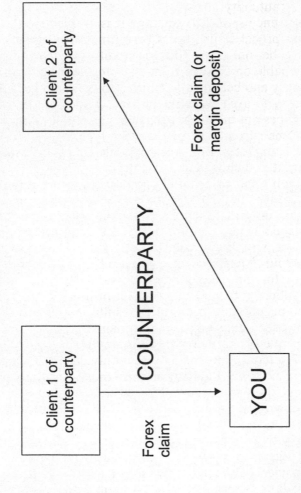

Client 2 of counterparty

Client 1 of counterparty

COUNTERPARTY

YOU

Forex claim

Forex claim (or margin deposit)

*Source:* Allen & Overy

contracting as agents and require each party to hold its claims for its own account.

## 11. MULTILATERAL NETTING

Under a system of multilateral netting, market participants agree that, not only will bilateral claims between mutual counterparties be netted out, but also that all claims owed between one party and all other counterparties are to be netted so that each party owes or is owed only a single balance to or by the rest of the market. The commonest application of multilateral netting is to payment systems, but these schemes exist in other contexts, *eg* airline netting and electricity pool netting.

From the legal point of view, if the netting does not take place prior to an insolvency petition against a relevant participant, the netting is vulnerable because the multilateral netting inevitably involves a set-off of non-mutual claims. A non-mutual set-off always leads to the divestment of the asset of an insolvent contrary to insolvency law and the use of one person's money to pay another's debt. The British Eagle case in 1975 in England is only one example of the nullification of an attempted multilateral set-off.

Techniques can be developed to mitigate this risk or avoid it altogether, *eg* by the use of cross-guarantees or a clearing-house acting as a principal on all market bargains.

If a clearing-house is used, all trade between market members are deemed to be trades with the clearing-house as principal. Thus if A agrees to sell to B, then this is treated as a sale by A to the clearing-house which in turn sells to B. The effect is that all trades which a defaulting member would otherwise have had with the other members – and which could not be netted on insolvency because of the lack of mutuality – become instead trades between the defaulter and the clearing-house which are mutual and hence eligible for netting. This mutualisation can result in a very substantial enhancement of netting (see Figure 6).

There are various routine contractual techniques whereby

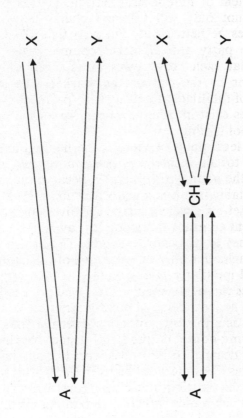

**Figure 6 Clearing-houses**

*Source:* Allen & Overy

trades between members can be converted into trades with the clearing-house, *eg* acceptance by conduct, agency or novation.

Since the clearing-house is principal on all transactions, it is usually essential for the members to provide it with credit support.

The insertion of a clearing-house as principal is now standard procedure in many organised futures markets and has recently been inaugurated for inter-bank foreign exchange.

# 12. INTER-GROUP AND INTER-BRANCH NETTING

Inter-group netting is the netting of contracts entered into by the creditor with one company in the counterparty's group against contracts entered into with another company in the same group, *eg* parent and subsidiary.

This type of netting is universally ineffective on the insolvency of one of the companies, because the claims are not mutual (see section 10). But the necessary mutuality can be created by each company guaranteeing the other. These guarantees must of course be valid, *eg* by satisfying any corporate benefit requirement.

Inter-branch netting is the netting of contracts entered into by the creditor with different branches of the counterparty where the branches are not separate legal entities. There is no mutuality objection to this type of netting since the contracts are all with the same legal entity. But see below as to the position where the branches are in different jurisdictions.

# 13. GLOBAL INTER-BRANCH NETTING

Global inter-branch netting is the netting of contracts with different branches of the same counterparty in different countries, *eg* the netting of contracts with the head office of the counterparty in Ruritania as against contracts with a branch of the counterparty in Kinglandia.

If the branch is a separate subsidiary, then the netting is not possible because of lack of mutuality. A guarantee may resolve this problem.

In other cases, prudence requires that the laws of both countries should allow netting. One reason is that the insolvency laws of many countries require creditors to return to the insolvent estate any excess recoveries they obtained abroad which they would not have obtained in the local insolvency, so that the creditor who nets against the foreign branch validly in accordance with foreign insolvency laws, but in defiance of head office law, may be exposed to a recovery action in the jurisdiction of the head office. Another is that the rules governing international conflicts of law in insolvency matters are shifting and, in many jurisdictions, unresolved.

Even if both jurisdictions allow netting in the case of local transactions, it is necessary to establish that one of the jurisdictions does not override its normal validation of netting by insisting that local assets should be preserved for local creditors, notably the tax authorities and local employees. This might be relevant if, say, the contracts with the local branch produced a gain in favour of the branch, but the contracts with the foreign head office produced a loss payable to the creditor. If the creditor sought to set off the loss against the gain, the creditors of the local branch would be deprived of the gain.

Nationalistic policies favouring local creditors to the detriment of foreign creditors appear here and there (*eg* in Latin American countries), notwithstanding that they lead to discrimination against foreign creditors. The foreign creditor is discriminated against because he is deprived of a protection he would have had if he were a local creditor.

It will generally be found that a country which overrides its normal netting in this case has a strong protectionist policy and a weak set-off policy.

English insolvency law seeks to treat all creditors equally, whether English or foreign, and the case law involving global set-off supports a non-discriminatory approach. Netting is a strong English policy and insolvency discrimination against foreigners is consistently disapproved of in judicial pronouncements.

## 14. CROSS-PRODUCT NETTING

Cross-product netting is the netting of different types of contract, *eg* interest swaps and foreign exchange contracts.

Under English insolvency law, there is no objection to cross-product netting: the contracts do not have to be of the same type. This seems to be generally true in those countries which are sympathetic to netting.

Cross-product netting may be more problematic in jurisdictions which are hostile to netting, but which allow it in the case of connexity. This is because connexity may be more difficult to establish if the contracts are of a different order.

In the case of countries such as United States and Canada where netting is limited to specific transactions, the contracts must come within the applicable legislation.

## 15. CROSS-CURRENCY NETTING

In some jurisdictions – which otherwise permit insolvency set-off – it needs to be considered whether set-off is permitted if the obligations are payable in different currencies. Many commercial countries compulsorily convert claims owing by the insolvent into local currency, so that the claim owing to the insolvent is in a different (foreign) currency.

English insolvency law permits cross-currency set-off: both claims must be converted into sterling at the date of the winding-up order. There appears to be a measure of international consensus on this point in legal doctrine in a number of jurisdictions which favour insolvency set-off. Currency conversion by contract could be considered.

# 16. SPECIAL COUNTERPARTIES

Netting is primarily, but not exclusively, governed by insolvency law. In many countries, the insolvency regime may differ according to the character of the debtor. In particular, there may be special rules for banks, insurance companies, statutory public companies, savings institutions and municipalities. These rules may override normal creditor protections in the interests of rehabilitating the debtor.

There is no special regime in England for bank insolvencies which is relevant in this context. The position with regard to other special institutions, such as insurance companies, is detailed. The availability of netting against non-corporate trusts, such as unit trusts, is also a specialist subject, largely because set-off is replaced by the more refined concept of retainer.

Netting against sovereign states is a matter for ordinary contract law since states are not subject to forced bankruptcy laws. In the senior jurisdictions, a state may usually waive sovereign immunity and, in any event, immunity should not normally be a bar to netting. This is because netting does not involve judicial action or judicial enforcement against a sovereign. This, at least, is the position under English law.

# 17. MARGIN

Transactions in organised markets are usually subject to a margin requirement whereby traders must provide the counterparty (or the clearing-house) with security to cover exposures. The security may take the form of initial margin plus variation margin: variation margin must be provided if there are fluctuations in market rates which increase the exposure.

Margin may be by way of cash deposit, securities or letters of credit. The international legal regime governing security falls outside the scope of this chapter, except in noting that the rules are important and much more labyrinthine than the netting rules. Repos have been developed in an attempt to circumvent some of the inconveniences of security law and their efficacy is itself a large field.

# 18. POST-INSOLVENCY CONTRACTS

In most jurisdictions which permit insolvency set-off, there is an additional rule preventing build-ups of set-offs in the twilight period. For example, a debtor owing 100 to the prospective bankrupt buys a claim of 100 owed by the bankrupt to the creditor. The debtor then has a set-off. The creditor is content to sell at a discount since he can expect only a tiny dividend on his claim.

Usually, the set-off statute prohibits a set-off resulting from this transaction after the parties become aware of the bankrupt's financial difficulties, sometimes with a maximum suspect period, *eg* six months. The English suspect period in the third paragraph of Rule 4.90 of the Insolvency Rules 1986 is very short – notice of petition or of a notice summoning a creditor's meeting.

Occasionally, the principle applies not only to acquired debts, but also to new debts contracted with the bankrupt. This is not considered a significant commercial risk because it appears to be usually – if not always – the case that the third party must be aware of the counterparty's actual insolvency or of steps to commence proceedings.

Contracts entered after insolvency petition may be vulnerable, even if the creditor acts in good faith. English case law suggests that creditors acting in good faith without notice will be protected but the present guidelines are insufficient to assert this. This point is not generally regarded as a serious commercial risk.

Some insolvency jurisdictions backdate the opening of insolvency proceedings to zero hour on the day of the court order opening the insolvency. Any payments made on that day by the insolvent before the bankruptcy order, but after zero, may be recoverable. The point affects settlement risk. English compulsory liquidations commence at the time when the petition is presented and the zero rule does not apply.

# 19. PREFERENCES

As mentioned, insolvency preference rules require the disgorge by a creditor of transfers and payments to him which are made by a debtor while actually insolvent in the suspect period and which put the creditor in a better position than he would otherwise have been and hence prejudice other creditors.

Under English insolvency law compensating contracts entered into in the suspect period which in fact turn out in improving the creditor's position on insolvency of the counterparty should not be capable of being set aside as a preference if they are at market value when entered into. A market value contract does not improve position – this will only occur if subsequently there are fluctuations in values. In any event, the counterparty will generally lack the necessary preferential intent in entering into the contract.

# 20. MISCELLANEOUS

Some netting contracts set out a method of calculating losses and gains on a close-out. In England, liquidated damages clauses which are a genuine pre-estimate of losses likely to be suffered on a breach are not a penalty: the rule is liberal and these clauses are not struck down unless clearly excessive. There appears to be general agreement on this issue amongst developed legal systems.

But compulsory conversions of foreign currency into local currency on insolvency might in some countries (including England) substitute the statutory rate of exchange for the contract rate. But the statutory rate is usually a market rate, so that this seems technical.

Gaming laws in some countries might call into question contracts for differences.

Consideration should be given to the position on an amalgamation of the counterparty by fusion and appropriate clauses introduced.

## 21. THE WAY FORWARD

It is difficult for financial institutions to carry on a global business where legal rules are a mosaic or a patchwork of national colours. Traders cannot be expected to be lawyers as well.

Any ideal international regime, would be consistent, harmonious, natural and simple. It would not require constant reference to lawyers. It would not require legal device or artifice in netting contracts. But of course the ideal is difficult to achieve internationally.

The insolvency laws of a jurisdiction will naturally reflect wider policies, of which the availability of netting is only one. But for states which are persuaded of the merits of netting, or which wish to ensure that their institutions are not disadvantaged, there seem to be at least two possible legal approaches.

Under the first approach, netting law would be the same for all contracts and for everybody, big bank or small trader, corporation or individual. The advantages of this approach are that it is non-discriminatory, can meet market changes without the need for amendment, and is simple to understand. This is the English approach and (it is believed) the approach adopted in such countries as Germany, the Netherlands, Japan, Switzerland and Sweden. On occasion, the law may have to be changed by legislation in specific and narrow areas to iron out inconsistencies, *eg* to neutralise the impact on netting of a rehabilitative or composition law, to correct an ambiguity, or to bring special counterparties within the netting law.

Under the second approach, netting is treated as a privilege conferred only on certain institutions and certain types of contract, but not available to the citizen at large. This is the approach adopted in the United States, Canada and Belgium. The advantage is that the state can continue to adhere to its general insolvency attitudes. Possible disadvantages are that the law is often complicated, particularly if the legislator is endeavouring to limit the scope of the privilege, that the rules might be over-rigid and ill-equipped to absorb rapid market developments, that the world still has the mosaic problem, that statutory particularity sometimes leads to ambiguity and that the scope of the relaxation is too narrow. But on the other hand, this may be the only realistic solution in countries which desire to protect their major markets against systemic risk, but have a deep-rooted and long historical tradition against set-off and netting on insolvency and wish to maintain that tradition for the ordinary case.

While it is unsafe for an English lawyer to trespass on the legal domains of others, it is believed that the present situation may be summed up tentatively as follows:

(a) The following jurisdictions (amongst others) allow default netting as against banks and corporates generally without discrimination on final bankruptcy:

| | |
|---|---|
| Australia | Italy |
| Austria | Japan |
| Cayman Islands | Netherlands |
| Denmark | Scotland |
| England | Singapore |
| Germany | Sweden |
| Hong Kong | Switzerland |

(b) The following countries might not permit default netting on bankruptcy (except in the case of connexity) but have specific statutory exceptions for special cases:

Belgium
Canada
United States

(c) The following countries (amongst others) might not permit default netting on bankruptcy except in the case of connexity

France (no rescission, no insolvency set-off)
Greece (no insolvency set-off)
Luxembourg (no insolvency set-off)
Portugal (no insolvency set-off)
Spain (no insolvency set-off)

# INDEX